Steve Harrison

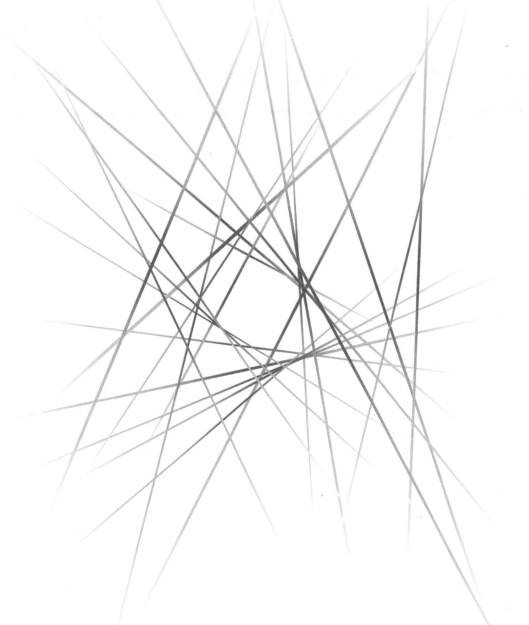

ESSENTIALS

AQA

GCSE French

Revision Guide

Contents

Revised

4   Exam Overview

Essential French

6   Essential French

Lifestyle 1

10   Personal Information and Family

12   Family and Friends

16   Relationships with Family and Friends

18   Future Plans – Marriage and Partnership

20   Social Issues

22   Practice Questions

Lifestyle 2

24   Healthy and Unhealthy Lifestyles

32   Sports and Exercise

34   Practice Questions

Leisure

36   Free Time Activities

40   Shopping, Money, Fashion and Trends

44   New Technology

48   Holidays

54   Weather

56   Getting Around

58   Practice Questions

Contents

Home and Environment

60 Home and Local Area

66 Being Environmentally Friendly

68 Current Problems Facing the Planet

70 Celebrations in the Home

74 Practice Questions

Work and Education

76 What School is Like

80 Pressures and Problems at School

82 Current and Future Jobs

88 Practice Questions

90 Word Bank

92 Answers

96 Index

Exam Overview

Listening

You usually have five minutes to look through the exam paper before the test starts. Use this time sensibly by checking what topics have come up and making notes on the paper to help you.

- Read the questions carefully. Sometimes a single word can make a big difference, for example, the questions, 'What subjects does he like?' and 'What subjects does he dislike?' need very different answers.
- Don't panic if you're unable to answer the question the first time you hear the recording. Remember, you'll hear the recordings twice.
- You aren't expected to understand everything that you hear in the recording. You may just need to work out the gist of what's being said.
- Never leave a blank space – that always scores zero. So, if you're genuinely stuck, try to make a sensible guess.
- Try to visualise words when you hear them. Words that would be obvious in a reading exam, such as **le train**, **l'athlétisme** or **le théâtre** sound very different in spoken French.

- Listen out for negatives, which can catch you out particularly in the listening part of the exam.
- Don't assume that the first word you hear is the correct one. For example, if you hear, '**Je ne vais plus au collège en voiture, j'y vais en bus**' and the question asks how the person gets to school, the answer is not 'by car', even though you hear the word **voiture**.

Reading

As with the listening part of the exam, having a good knowledge of vocabulary is essential. This is even more crucial in reading where examiners will expect you to deal with some unfamiliar words because you can use communication strategies to work out the meaning. For example, if you know that **chanter** means 'to sing', you'll be expected to know that **chanteur** means 'singer' because you will have met other words ending in **-eur**, such as **travailleur**, **acteur** and **vendeur**.

- Watch out for tenses by looking at endings carefully. **J'aimais** is past tense (I used to like) but **j'aimerais** is the conditional tense and means 'I would like'.
- Some high frequency words, such as **souvent**, **toujours**, **jamais**, **sauf** and **encore** can alter the meaning of a sentence. Make sure you read each sentence carefully.
- In questions aimed at the highest grades, you may have to come to conclusions or draw inferences from what you read. For example: '**Il ne fait pas toujours ses devoirs, il trouve les maths difficiles et il ne s'entend pas bien avec les profs**' means that this person is probably having problems at school.
- When revising, try to learn vocabulary in categories so that you can see the connections between words. If the answer to a question that asks the person's favourite hobby is 'reading', the word **la lecture** may not even be there at all. Words such as **un roman** (a novel) or **le journal** (newspaper) might give you the answer instead.

Speaking

The speaking exam is part of the controlled assessment. You'll have to produce two pieces of spoken assessment during the GCSE course, which will be marked by your French teacher. Each assessment should be between 4 and 6 minutes long.

Your teacher can help you to plan what you want to talk about. You are allowed notes with you when you do the test, but these cannot be more than 40 words long and must not contain any conjugated verbs (i.e. **aller** is fine, but **je vais** or **je suis allé** are not). You can devise your own task or use one provided by AQA. Check with your teacher about exactly what is allowed.

- Be aware that at some point in the test your teacher will ask you a question that you haven't prepared an answer for.
- Make sure that what you intend to say contains plenty of opinions and reasons to make it more personal.
- Try to cover a variety of time frames, for example, saying what you've done recently to illustrate your point.
- When revising, see if you can ask someone to record some key phrases for you – in French it's easy to mispronounce words if you only revise by reading

your notes. It's important to avoid the temptation to pronounce the **-s** at the end of words like **dans**.
- Avoid answers that are too short; always try to develop what you say. But, don't try to give overlong answers that sound like pre-rehearsed presentations.
- Try to include some longer sentences by using connectives, such as **parce que**, **qui**, **où**, **cependant**, etc.

Writing

The writing exam is part of the controlled assessment. You'll have to produce two pieces of written work during the GCSE course. These will be done in school and will be marked by AQA.

To gain the very highest marks these two pieces should come to about 600 words overall.

You can do a task devised by AQA, by your teacher or by yourself. Check with your teacher that your choice of topic is suitable. You may produce a draft and ask your teacher to comment on it using an official feedback form.

- You should include opinions, reasons and justifications wherever possible and use a variety of tenses.
- You're allowed to use a dictionary when writing the final version of your work under supervision. Try to use the dictionary only to check spellings and genders. Avoid the temptation to look up new words that you don't know as this can lead to misunderstandings and errors.
- You need to include as much complexity as possible in your work, i.e. longer sentences, complex grammatical structures and a variety of vocabulary.
- Make use of adverbs, adjectives and pronouns where you can.

For further information, see www.aqa.org.uk

Essential French

Numbers

0	**zéro**	22	**vingt-deux**	about 10	**une dizaine**
1	**un**	23	**vingt-trois**	about 20	**une vingtaine**
2	**deux**	30	**trente**		
3	**trois**	31	**trente et un**	first	**le premier / la première**
4	**quatre**	35	**trente-cinq**	second	**le deuxième / la deuxième /**
5	**cinq**	40	**quarante**		**le second / la seconde**
6	**six**	50	**cinquante**	third	**le troisième / la troisième**
7	**sept**	60	**soixante**	fourth	**le quatrième / la quatrième**
8	**huit**	70	**soixante-dix**		
9	**neuf**	71	**soixante et onze**		
10	**dix**	72	**soixante-douze**		
11	**onze**	73	**soixante-treize**		
12	**douze**	80	**quatre-vingts**		
13	**treize**	81	**quatre-vingt-un**		
14	**quatorze**	82	**quatre-vingt-deux**		
15	**quinze**	90	**quatre-vingt-dix**		
16	**seize**	91	**quatre-vingt-onze**		
17	**dix-sept**	95	**quatre-vingt-quinze**		
18	**dix-huit**	99	**quatre-vingt-dix-neuf**		
19	**dix-neuf**	100	**cent**		
20	**vingt**	101	**cent un**		
21	**vingt et un**	1000	**mille**		

Months

janvier	January	**mai**	May	**septembre**	September
février	February	**juin**	June	**octobre**	October
mars	March	**juillet**	July	**novembre**	November
avril	April	**août**	August	**décembre**	December

Days and Dates

lundi	Monday
mardi	Tuesday
mercredi	Wednesday
jeudi	Thursday
vendredi	Friday
samedi	Saturday
dimanche	Sunday

Quelle est la date aujourd'hui?
What's today's date?

Aujourd'hui, c'est mardi douze juillet.
Today is Tuesday the 12th of July.

C'est le trente octobre mille neuf cent quatre-vingt-seize.
It's the 30th October 1996.

Essential French

The Time

Quelle heure est-il? What time is it?	→	Il est... midi minuit une heure trois heures cinq heures cinq six heures et quart dix heures et demie onze heures moins vingt midi moins le quart du matin / soir de l'après-midi	It is... midday midnight 1 o'clock 3 o'clock 5 past 5 quarter past 6 half past ten 20 to 11 quarter to 12 in the morning / evening in the afternoon

The French tend to use the 24-hour clock more than we do, for example:

- **Treize heures dix** 1.10pm
- **Vingt et une heures** 9pm
- **Seize heures trente** 4.30pm
- **Une heure quarante** 1.40am

A quelle heure? At what time?	→	A minuit et demi. A six heures du soir. A neuf heures moins vingt-cinq.	At half past midnight. At 6 o'clock in the evening. At 25 to 9.

Colours

C'est de quelle couleur? What colour is it?	→	rouge bleu vert jaune blanc noir gris orange	red blue green yellow white black grey orange	**brun** **marron** **rose** **roux** **blond** **violet** **bleu clair** **bleu foncé**	brown brown pink ginger (red hair) blonde purple light blue dark blue

The Alphabet

A	as in **samedi**	J	as in **j'y vais**	S	as in **une promesse**
B	as in **un bébé**	K	as in **un coca**	T	as in **une tasse de thé**
C	as in **c'est**	L	as in **belle**	U	as in **quel âge as-tu?**
D	as in **un détective**	M	as in **j'aime**	V	as in **un vélo**
E	as in **il pleut**	N	as in **moyenne**	W	say **dou-bleu vé**
F	as in **efficace**	O	as in **un gâteau**	X	as in **Astérix**
G	as in **j'ai**	P	as in **un canapé**	Y	say **ee grec**
H	as in **une vache**	Q	as in **vaincu**	Z	say **zed**
I	as in **midi**	R	as in **Air France**		

Comment vous appelez-vous?
Comment ça s'écrit?

What's your name? How do you spell it?

Je m'appelle Vasse. Ça s'écrit V-A-deux S-E.

My name is Vasse. It's spelt V-A-double S-E.

Essential French

Being Polite

There are two words for 'you' in French: **tu** and **vous**.

You can use **tu** when speaking to a friend, a member of your family or an animal. For example:

- **Où habites-tu?**
  Where do you live?

If you're speaking to more than one friend, or several relatives or animals, use **vous**.
For example:

- **Où habitez-vous?**
  Where do you live?

You must also use **vous** if you're speaking to one person politely, such as a waiter, a shop assistant or a stranger. For example:

- **Bonjour, monsieur. Avez-vous des bananes?**
  Hello, sir. Have you any bananas?
- **Mademoiselle, l'addition, s'il vous plaît.**
  Miss, the bill, please.

There are two ways to say 'please':

- **s'il te plaît** is used for someone you address with **tu**.
- **s'il vous plaît** is the polite form.

Salut can be used for 'hello' or 'goodbye', when you're being informal.

Greetings

À bientôt	See you soon	**Bonne idée**	Good idea
À demain	See you tomorrow	**Bonne nuit**	Goodnight
À tout à l'heure	See you very soon	**Bonnes vacances**	Have a good holiday
Allô	Hello (on the phone)	**Bonsoir**	Good evening
Amitiés	Best wishes	**Bravo**	Well done
Bien sûr	Of course	**Ça va?**	How are you?
Bienvenue	Welcome	**Excusez-moi**	Excuse me
Bon anniversaire	Happy birthday	**Félicitations**	Congratulations
Bon appétit	Enjoy your meal	**Pardon**	Excuse me / sorry
Bon voyage	Have a good journey	**Santé!**	Cheers!
Bonne année	Happy New Year	**D'accord**	OK
Bonne chance	Good luck		

Useful Phrases

Je ne sais pas	I don't know	**Je veux bien**	Yes please	**Où sont les toilettes?**	Where are the toilets?
Je ne comprends pas	I don't understand	**Non merci**	No thanks	**C'est gentil**	That's kind
Comment?	Pardon?	**De rien**	Don't mention it	**Quel dommage**	What a shame
Désolé	Sorry	**Un instant!**	Wait a bit!	**Il ne fallait pas**	You shouldn't have
C'est vrai	That's true	**Attends!**	Wait!		
Ce n'est pas vrai	That's not true	**Au secours!**	Help!	**Oh là là!**	Dear me!
Vraiment?	Really?	**Au feu!**	Fire!	**Zut!**	Blast!
Pouvez-vous m'aider?	Can you help me?	**Au voleur!**	Stop, thief!		
Tout de suite	Straightaway	**C'est sûr?**	Is that definite?		
		Je vous en prie	Don't mention it		

Essential French

Question Words

Quand?	When?	**Où?**	Where?	
Que? /	What?	**Pourquoi?**	Why?	
Qu'est-ce que?		**Comment?**	How?	
Qui?	Who?	**Combien?**	How many / much?	
Quel / quelle / quels / quelles?	What? / Which?	**Combien de temps?**	How long?	

Note this use of **comment**:
- **Comment est ta maison?**
  What's your house like?

Conjunctions and Connectives

à cause de	because of	**d'un côté**	on the one hand	**par contre**	on the other hand
à part	apart from	**d'un autre côté**	on the other hand	**par exemple**	for example
alors	so	**donc**	so, therefore	**pendant que**	while
aussi	also, too	**ensuite**	afterwards	**pourtant**	yet
aussitôt que	as soon as	**en revanche**	on the other hand	**puis**	then
car	since	**évidemment**	obviously	**puisque**	since
cependant	however	**et**	and	**sans doute**	probably
c'est-à-dire	that's to say	**grâce à**	thanks to	**sauf**	except
comme	as, like	**lorsque / quand**	when	**sinon**	if not
d'abord	firstly	**même si**	even if	**tandis que**	whereas
d'ailleurs	moreover	**ou**	or	**y compris**	including
dû à	owing to	**parce que**	because		

Common Abbreviations

CDI (centre de documentation et d'information)	school library	**SAMU (service d'aide médicale d'urgence)**	ambulance service
CES (collège d'enseignement secondaire)	secondary school	**SIDA**	AIDS
EMT (éducation manuelle et technique)	technology	**SNCF (société nationale des chemins de fer français)**	French rail
EPS (éducation physique et sportive)	PE	**TGV (train à grande vitesse)**	high speed train
		TVA (taxe sur la valeur ajoutée)	VAT
HLM (habitation à loyer modéré)	social housing	**VTT (vélo tout terrain)**	mountain bike

Quick Test

1 Say / write it in English:
  a) C'est mercredi six juillet deux mille huit.
  b) L'heure est dix heures quinze du matin.

2 Say / write it in French:
  a) My name is Pierre. It's spelt P-i-e-r-r-e.
  b) Excuse me, where is the school library?

Personal Information and Family

Members of the Family and Pets

Here are some useful words for describing members of your family and your pets:

le bébé	baby		**la maman**	mum
le chat	cat		**le mari**	husband
le cheval	horse		**la mère**	mother
le chien	dog		**l'oiseau**	bird
le cochon d'Inde	guinea pig		**l'oncle**	uncle
l'enfant	child		**le papa**	dad
la famille	family		**le / la partenaire**	partner
la femme	wife / woman		**le père**	father
la fille	daughter / girl		**le poisson rouge**	goldfish
le fils	son		**la sœur**	sister
le frère	brother		**la souris**	mouse
le garçon	boy		**la tante**	aunt
la grand-mère	grandmother		**le beau-père**	step-father / father-in-law
le grand-père	grandfather		**la belle-sœur**	step-sister / sister-in-law
les grands-parents	grandparents		**le demi-frère**	half-brother
l'homme	man		**la demi-sœur**	half-sister
le lapin	rabbit			

Gender, Singular and Plural

French nouns are either masculine or feminine. You can usually tell by the article in front of them what gender the words are.

Le **père** and le **frère** are masculine, as you would expect, but so are le **chat** and le **cheval**.

La **fille** and la **tante** are, of course, feminine, but so are la **famille** and la **souris**.

Le and la both change to les in the plural: les **frères**, les **sœurs**.

Un **chien** is masculine, but une **famille** is feminine.

Un and une both change to des in the plural: des **chiens**, des **familles**.

Look out for words beginning with a vowel or a silent **h**, e.g. l'oncle, l'homme. These are clearly masculine but l'oiseau is less obvious. When you see un oiseau, you'll realise that it's masculine.

To make a word plural, you usually add **-s** (but this is often silent in French):

- **Un chien** ➡ **deux chiens**
- **La fille** ➡ **des filles**

Words ending in **-s** don't change:

- **Un fils** ➡ **deux fils**

Words ending in **-eau** often add **-x**:

- **Un oiseau** ➡ **cinq oiseaux**

Words ending in **-al** change to **-aux**:

- **Un animal** ➡ **des animaux**
- **Un cheval** ➡ **trois chevaux**.

Personal Information and Family

Talking about Yourself

Here are some useful expressions you could use to introduce yourself:

J'... / I...	→	ai / have
Je... / I...	→	m'appelle / suis / am called / am
Il / Elle / He / She	→	s'appelle / est / a / is called / is / has
Ils / Elles / They	→	s'appellent / sont / ont / are called / are / have

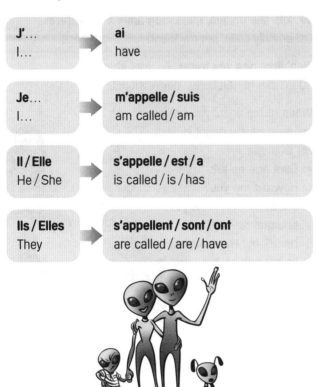

Mon prénom est... et mon nom de famille est...
My first name is... and my surname is...

J'ai un frère et une sœur.
I have one brother and one sister.

J'ai deux sœurs, mais je n'ai pas de frères.
I have two sisters, but I don't have any brothers.

Je suis fils / fille unique.
I'm an only child.

Mes frères s'appellent... et...
My brothers are called... and...

J'ai quinze ans.
I'm fifteen.

Mon père a quarante ans.
My dad's forty.

How to Say 'My' and 'Your'

To say 'my' in French, you need to know if the word you're describing is masculine, feminine or plural, then use **mon**, **ma** or **mes**:

* **Mon père s'appelle Paul et ma mère s'appelle Pauline. Mes parents sont sympa.**
  My father's called Paul and my mother's called Pauline. My parents are nice.

To say 'your' in French, use **ton**, **ta** or **tes**:

* **J'adore ton frère mais ta sœur est pénible.**
  I love your brother but your sister gets on my nerves.
* **Tes grands-parents sont gentils.**
  Your grandparents are kind.

Be careful with **son**, **sa** and **ses**, which can mean 'his' or 'her' depending on what you're talking about:

* **Ma sœur a un chien. Son chien s'appelle Bruno.**
  My sister has a dog. Her dog's called Bruno.
* **Mon frère a une souris. Sa souris s'appelle Mimi.**
  My brother has a mouse. His mouse is called Mimi.

*N.B. Feminine words beginning with a vowel or silent 'h' take **mon**, **ton** and **son**, e.g. **mon amie, son école**.*

Quick Test

1. Say / write it in English:
   a) **Mon père a trente-neuf ans.**
   b) **Ma sœur a un lapin.**
   c) **J'ai deux sœurs, mais je n'ai pas de frères.**
2. Say / write it in French:
   a) My father is forty five.
   b) My mother has a brother.
   c) I am an only child.

Family and Friends

'Avoir' and 'Être'

Avoir and **être** are very important verbs. They're very useful when you want to describe yourself or someone else. Here they are in full:

Avoir (to have)	
J'ai	I have
Tu as	You have
Il / Elle a	He / She has
Nous avons	We have
Vous avez	You have
Ils / Elles ont	They have
Être (to be)	
Je suis	I am
Tu es	You are
Il / Elle est	He / She is
Nous sommes	We are
Vous êtes	You are
Ils / Elles sont	They are

Je suis anglais, mais ma mère est française.
I'm English, but my mother is French.

Je suis fille unique, mais mon amie a trois frères.
I'm an only child, but my friend has 3 brothers.

Je n'aime pas ses frères, ils sont stupides.
I don't like her brothers, they're stupid.

When giving ages, you use **avoir**, not **être**, as you might expect. For example:

- **Quel âge as-tu?**
  How old are you?
- **J'ai seize ans, mais j'ai presque dix-sept ans.**
  I'm 16, but I'm nearly 17.
- **Ils ont quinze ans tous les deux.**
  They're both 15.

Describing People

Here are some useful expressions for describing your own and other people's appearances.

Je suis petit / petite et maigre.
I'm small and thin.

Il est grand. Elle est grande et mince.
He is tall. She is tall and slim.

Ils sont de taille moyenne.
They are of medium height.

J'ai les cheveux blonds et bouclés.
I have blond, curly hair.

Elle a les cheveux bruns et raides.
She has brown, straight hair.

Il a les cheveux roux et les yeux bleus.
He has ginger hair and blue eyes.

Mon frère a les yeux verts.
My brother has green eyes.

Ma sœur a les yeux gris.
My sister has grey eyes.

Mon père porte des lunettes.
My father wears glasses.

Ma mère a les cheveux longs mais j'ai les cheveux courts.
My mother has long hair but I have short hair.

Mon amie a les cheveux mi-longs.
My friend has medium-length hair.

Ma sœur est jolie, mais mon frère est laid.
My sister is pretty, but my brother is ugly.

-er Verbs

Most verbs in French are **-er** verbs, so you need to make sure you know all the correct endings.

The verb **porter** is an **-er** verb. Here's the present tense of **porter** in full:

Je porte	I wear / I'm wearing
Tu portes	You wear / you're wearing
Il / Elle porte	He / She wears / is wearing
Nous portons	We wear / we're wearing
Vous portez	You wear / you're wearing
Ils / Elles portent	They wear / they're wearing

Elle porte des lunettes.
She wears glasses.

Here are some other **-er** verbs:

préférer	
e.g. **Je préfère**	I prefer
aimer	
e.g. **J'aime**	I like
détester	
e.g. **Je déteste**	I hate
adorer	
e.g. **J'adore**	I love
habiter	
e.g. **J'habite**	I live

Finding Out About Others

As well as telling other people about yourself and your family, you'll want to find out about the person you're talking to. So, you'll want to ask questions like these:

Comment t'appelles-tu?
What's your name?

Quel âge as-tu?
How old are you?

Quelle est la date de ton anniversaire?
When's your birthday?

Où habites-tu?
Where do you live?

De quelle couleur sont tes yeux?
What colour are your eyes?

Comment sont tes cheveux?
What's your hair like?

De quelle couleur est-il?
What colour is it?

Tu as des frères ou des sœurs?
Do you have any brothers or sisters?

Comment s'appelle ton frère?
What's your brother's name?

Quel âge a-t-il?
How old is he?

Comment est-il?
What does he look like?

Quelle est la date de son anniversaire?
When is his birthday?

Quick Test

1 Say / write it in English:
   a) Mon père a les cheveux courts.
   b) Ma mère porte des lunettes.
   c) Je suis de taille moyenne.

2 Say / write it in French:
   a) My father has long hair.
   b) I have brown hair and blue eyes.
   c) What's your brother's name?

Family and Friends

Adjectives

Adjectives are very useful words for describing someone's appearance or personality. Remember, in French, the ending of the adjective depends on whether the person you're describing is masculine or feminine, or whether you're describing one person or more. For example:

- **Mon père est grand**   My father is tall.
- **Ma mère est grande**   My mother is tall.
- **Mes parents sont grands**   My parents are tall.

Adjectives ending in **-x** change to **-se** in the feminine, for example:

- **Mon frère est paresseux et ma sœur est paresseuse, elle aussi.**
  My brother is lazy and my sister is lazy too.

Adjectives ending in **-f** change to -**ve** in the feminine, for example:

- **Mon cousin est sportif et ma tante est sportive, elle aussi.**
  My cousin is sporty and my aunt is sporty too.

Adjectives ending in **-n** tend to double the **n** and add **-e** in the feminine (**-nne**), for example:

- **Mon petit neveu est mignon et ma nièce est mignonne, elle aussi.**
  My little nephew is cute and my niece is cute too.

Describing Personality

Here are some useful adjectives for describing people's personalities:

sympa	nice, friendly	**drôle**	witty	**plein / pleine de vie**	full of life
casse-pieds	a nuisance	**patient / patiente**	patient	**sérieux / sérieuse**	serious
gentil / gentille	kind	**timide**	shy	**bavard(e)**	talkative,
impatient / impatiente	impatient	**poli / polie**	polite		chatty
généreux / généreuse	generous	**égoïste**	selfish	**travailleur(-euse)**	hard-working
impoli / impolie	impolite	**sévère**	strict	**maladroit(e)**	clumsy
amusant / amusante	funny	**intelligent / intelligente**	clever	**vif / vive**	lively
méchant / méchante	naughty	**ennuyeux / ennuyeuse**	boring		

Useful Verbs

Je... I...				
	bavarde avec...	chat with	**ne peux pas supporter**...	can't stand...
	m'entends bien avec...	get on well with	**déteste**...	hate...
	ne m'entends pas bien avec...	don't get on well with...	**me confie à**...	confide in...
	me dispute avec...	argue with...	**me méfie de**...	don't trust...
	tombe amoureux / amoureuse de...	fall in love with...		

Je déteste mon frère parce qu'il est paresseux.
I hate my brother because he's lazy.

Je ne peux pas supporter l'ami de mon frère parce qu'il est égoïste et ennuyeux.
I can't stand my brother's friend because he's selfish and boring.

Je bavarde souvent avec mes parents et je me confie à ma mère.
I often chat to my parents and I confide in my mother.

Comparing People

You can make comparisons by using one of the following three words with an adjective:

- **plus** more
- **moins** less
- **aussi** as

Mon frère est plus sportif que ma sœur.
My brother is more sporty than my sister.

Ma mère est plus généreuse que mon père.
My mother is more generous than my father.

Mon ami est moins bête que mon frère.
My friend is less stupid than my brother.

Ma sœur est aussi intelligente que moi.
My sister is as clever as me.

The French for 'better' is **meilleur(e)**. For example:
- **Mon ami est un meilleur chanteur que moi.**
  My friend is a better singer than me.

But with a verb, use **mieux** for 'better'. For example:
- **Mon ami chante mieux que moi.**
  My friend sings better than me.

To say 'the best', use **le meilleur, la meilleure** or **les meilleurs (les meilleures)**. For example:
- **Bolton Wanderers est la meilleure équipe de foot du monde.**
  Bolton Wanderers is the best football team in the world.

Pire is the French for 'worse' / 'worst'. For example:
- **Il chante pire que moi.**
  He sings worse than I do.

Intensifiers

Vary what you say by using intensifiers when you're describing people's personalities:

- **très** very
- **trop** too
- **assez** fairly
- **un peu** a (little) bit

Mon ami est très généreux, mais de temps en temps il est un peu impatient.
My friend is very generous, but sometimes he's a bit impatient.

Ma copine est assez amusante, mais elle peut être trop pleine de vie.
My friend is quite funny, but she can be too lively.

Useful Words

aîné(e)	older
cadet(te)	younger
le cousin	male cousin
la cousine	female cousin
un jumeau	male twin
une jumelle	female twin
le neveu	nephew
la nièce	niece
le petit-fils	grandson
la petite-fille	grand-daughter

Quick Test

1. Say / write it in English:
   a) **Je suis gentil et amusant.**
   b) **Ma sœur est intelligente et timide.**
   c) **Mes parents sont sérieux et impatients.**
2. Say / write it in French:
   a) My father is clever, but a bit serious.
   b) My brother is lazier than me.
   c) My sister is less selfish than my brother.

Relationships with Family and Friends

Relationships with Other People

bavarder	to chat	connaître	to know	se mettre en colère	to get angry
critiquer	to criticise	s'entendre avec	to get on with	réfléchir	to think about
divorcer	to divorce	s'habituer à	to get used to	rêver	to dream
épouser	to marry	se débrouiller	to cope, to get by	pleurer	to cry
se marier avec	to get married to	compter sur	to rely on	rire	to laugh
se confier à	to confide in	gêner	to embarrass	sourire	to smile

Reflexive Verbs

Some verbs are **reflexive verbs** because you need to use a pronoun when you use the verb. Here is the verb **se disputer** (to argue) with the correct pronouns in full:

- **Je me dispute avec mon frère.**
  I argue with my brother.
- **Est-ce que tu te disputes avec tes parents?**
  Do you argue with your parents?
- **Elle se dispute tout le temps avec ses copines.**
  She's always arguing with her friends.
- **Nous nous disputons souvent.**
  We often argue.

- **Vous vous disputez avec vos sœurs?**
  Do you argue with your sisters?
- **Ils se disputent au sujet de l'argent.**
  They argue about money.

Some reflexive verbs are used in descriptions of daily routine, for example:

- **Je me lève à 7 heures, je me lave et je me brosse les dents. Le soir, je me couche à 22h30.**
  I get up at 7 o'clock, have a wash and brush my teeth. In the evening, I go to bed at 10.30pm.

Talking about Friends and Family

amoureux(-euse)	in love	jeune	young	la naissance	birth
le bonheur	happiness	heureux(-euse)	happy	un petit ami	boyfriend
célibataire	single	malheureux(-euse)	unhappy	une petite amie	girlfriend
un copain	male friend	marrant(e)	funny	séparé(e)	separated
une copine	female friend	mort(e)	dead	seul(e)	alone / lonely
divorcé(e)	divorced	né(e)	born	veuf / veuve	widower / widow

Mon ami est compréhensif et aimable.
My friend is understanding and nice.

Ma petite amie est jolie et marrante et je peux me confier à elle.
My girlfriend is pretty and funny and I can confide in her.

Mon meilleur ami est très fidèle et je peux toujours compter sur lui.
My best friend is very loyal and I can always rely on him.

Ma meilleure copine ne se met jamais en colère et elle ne se dispute pas avec moi.
My best friend never gets angry and doesn't argue with me.

Mes parents critiquent mes vêtements et ils ne s'entendent pas avec mes amis.
My parents criticise my clothes and they don't get on with my friends.

Je connais mon frère. Il est trop impatient. Il parle avant de réfléchir.
I know my brother. He's too impatient. He speaks without thinking.

Relationships with Family and Friends

-re Verbs

The verb **s'entendre** (to get on) is an -re verb, as well as being a reflexive verb. The endings aren't the same as for -er verbs. Here it is in the present tense:

- **Je m'entends avec mes parents.**
  I get on with my parents.
- **Tu t'entends bien avec ton copain.**
  You get on well with your friend.
- **Elle s'entend bien avec sa sœur aînée.**
  She gets on well with her older sister.
- **Nous nous entendons à merveille.**
  We get on really well.

- **Vous vous entendez avec vos profs?**
  Do you get on well with your teachers?
- **Ils s'entendent la plupart du temps.**
  They get on well most of the time.

Note how **me**, **te** and **se** change to **m'**, **t'** and **s'** before a vowel.

Other common -re verbs are: **répondre** (to answer); **rendre** (to make + adjective) and **vendre** (to sell):

- **Elles me rendent heureux.**
  They make me happy.

Personal Qualities and Flaws

aimable	nice, pleasant, kind	**optimiste**	optimistic		
		poli	polite	**jaloux (se)**	jealous
amical(e)	friendly	**un sens de l'humour**	a sense of humour	**déprimé(e)**	depressed
animé(e)	lively			**impoli**	rude
compréhensif(-ive)	understanding	**tranquille**	calm, quiet	**méchant(e)**	nasty
fier (fière)	proud	**égoïste**	selfish	**pessimiste**	pessimistic
fou (folle)	mad	**fâché(e)**	angry	**triste**	sad

Special Pronouns

After words such as **avec** (with), **pour** (for) and **sans** (without), you need to use a special set of pronouns:

Moi	Me	**Nous**	Us
Toi	You (singular, friendly)	**Vous**	You (polite, plural)
Lui	Him	**Eux**	Them (masculine)
Elle	Her	**Elles**	Them (feminine)

For example:

- **Je m'entends avec eux.** — I get on with them.
- **Il est toujours là pour moi.** — He's always there for me.
- **Je ne peux pas vivre sans toi.** — I can't live without you.
- **Ils se disputent avec nous.** — They argue with us.

These pronouns are also used for emphasis so they're known as **emphatic pronouns**:

- **Toi, tu n'aimes pas les gens tristes.**
  You don't like sad people (you don't).
- **Moi, je suis travailleuse, mais mon frère est paresseux, lui.**
  (Me) I'm hard-working but my brother's lazy (he is).

Quick Test

1. Say / write it in English:
   a) Je m'entends bien avec elle.
   b) Ils se disputent souvent avec moi.
   c) Elle est amoureuse mais malheureuse.
2. Say / write it in French:
   a) My best friend is lively but a bit mad.
   b) I dream of marrying my girlfriend.
   c) My sister is more polite than my brother.

Future Plans – Marriage and Partnership

Using 'Aller' to Talk about Future Plans

To talk about what you're going to do in the future, you need to use the verb **aller** (to go). Here's the present tense of **aller** in full:

Je vais	I go, am going
Tu vas	You go, are going
Il / Elle va	He / She goes, is going
Nous allons	We go, are going
Vous allez	You go, are going
Ils / Elles vont	They go, are going

If you use the correct form of **aller** with the infinitive of the verb (e.g. **manger**, **aller**, **avoir**, **être**) it expresses future intentions. For example:

- **Je vais manger des frites.**
  I'm going to eat some chips.
- **Il va aller au cinéma.**
  He's going to go to the cinema.
- **Nous allons faire du shopping.**
  We're going to go shopping.
- **Les filles vont jouer au foot.**
  The girls are going to play football.

Talking About Future Plans

les enfants	children
épouser	to marry
féliciter	to congratulate
fêter	to celebrate
les fiançailles	engagement
heureux(-euse)	happy
le mariage	marriage
se marier avec…	to get married to…
la naissance	birth
les noces	wedding
le partenaire idéal	ideal partner
la partenaire idéale	ideal partner
le plaisir	pleasure
riche	rich
une alliance	wedding ring
l'amour	love
attendre	to wait
une bague	a ring
célèbre	famous

Je vais me marier à l'âge de 25 ans.
I'm going to get married at the age of 25.

Je ne vais pas me marier.
I'm not going to get married.

Je vais rester célibataire.
I'm going to stay single.

Tu vas avoir des enfants?
Are you going to have children?

Il veut avoir deux enfants – une fille et un garçon.
He wants to have two children – a girl and a boy.

Elle veut avoir des jumeaux.
She wants to have twins.

Sabine va épouser son partenaire idéal.
Sabine's going to marry her ideal partner.

Les filles vont devenir riches et célèbres.
The girls are going to become rich and famous.

-ir Verbs

A lot of French verbs end in **-ir**. Many (but not all) verbs ending in **-ir** are formed as follows:

Je chois**is**	I choose
Tu chois**is**	You choose
Il / Elle chois**it**	He / She chooses
Nous chois**issons**	We choose
Vous chois**issez**	You choose
Ils / Elles chois**issent**	They choose

Other **-ir** verbs that have the same endings include **finir** (to finish), **remplir** (to fill), **rougir** (to blush) and **saisir** (to seize). For example:

- **Les enfants finissent les devoirs.**
  The children are finishing the homework.
- **La fille rougit quand ses amies remarquent sa bague.**
  The girl blushes when her friends notice her ring.

Future Plans – Marriage and Partnership

Other Ways of Expressing Future Plans

As well as using the verb **aller** to convey future intentions, you could use these verbs:

Je veux	I want
Je voudrais	I'd like
Je pense	I'm thinking
Je rêve de	I dream of
J'ai l'intention de	I intend to
Je pourrais	I might / could
J'espère	I hope, am hoping

These verbs are all followed by the infinitive, for example:

- **A l'avenir, je veux épouser mon petit ami.**
  In the future, I want to marry my boyfriend.
- **Je voudrais avoir deux enfants.**
  I'd like to have two children.
- **Je pense demander ma copine en mariage.**
  I'm thinking of proposing to my girlfriend.
- **Je rêve de vivre à la campagne avec mon mari.**
  I dream of living in the country with my husband.
- **J'ai l'intention de voyager avant de me marier.**
  I intend to travel before I get married.
- **Dans le futur, je pourrais devenir riche et célèbre.**
  In the future, I might become rich and famous.
- **J'espère être heureuse.**
  I hope to be happy.

Useful Words

les adolescents	teenagers	**une fête familiale**	a family celebration
les adultes	adults	**le troisième âge**	older people
les jeunes	young people	**les rapports**	relationships
une famille nombreuse	a large family	**une mère célibataire**	single mother
les noces d'argent	silver wedding (anniversary)	**une famille monoparentale**	single-parent family
un / une bébé	baby	**le PACS**	civil partnership
enceinte	pregnant	**les vieux**	old people
un heureux événement	a happy event		

Tricky Adjectives

Watch out for these three adjectives: **vieux** (old), **beau** (beautiful) and **nouveau** (new). They have a special masculine form when the word begins with a vowel or a silent **h**.

un beau garçon	a good-looking boy
une belle fille	a beautiful / good-looking girl
un bel enfant	a beautiful child
un nouveau partenaire	a new partner
une nouvelle femme	a new wife
un nouvel ami	a new friend
un vieux monsieur	an old gentleman
une vieille dame	an old lady
un vieil homme	an old man

Quick Test

1. Say / write it in English:
   a) **Je vais épouser ma partenaire idéale.**
   b) **Je vais avoir trois enfants.**
   c) **Elle a l'intention de travailler aux États-Unis.**
2. Say / write it in French:
   a) My friend dreams of marrying Johnny Depp.
   b) My ideal partner is richer than me.
   c) Love is more important than a wedding.

Social Issues

Issues Affecting Society

Here are some useful words for describing issues that affect society:

les responsabilités	responsibilities				
le sondage	survey	**les exclus**	the excluded	**les réfugiés**	refugees
la manifestation	demonstration	**l'égalité**	equality	**la couleur de la peau**	skin colour
la guerre	war	**la famine**	famine		
le travail bénévole	voluntary work	**les sans-abris**	the homeless	**les droits**	rights
une organisation caritative	charity	**un SDF (sans domicile fixe)**	a homeless person	**la vérité**	truth
le SIDA	AIDS	**sans travail**	unemployed	**l'insécurité**	crime
la pauvreté	poverty	**le racisme**	racism	**un malfaiteur**	criminal
pauvre	poor	**Chrétien**	Christian	**un voyou**	thug
le chômage	unemployment	**Musulman**	Muslim	**le vandalisme**	vandalism
les dettes	debts	**la discrimination**	discrimination	**la violence**	violence
les défavorisés	those less fortunate	**les immigrés**	immigrants	**le vol**	theft
				le voleur	thief

'Il Faut'

The verb **falloir** (to be necessary) is only ever used in the **il** form. It's very useful when saying something 'must be done'. For example:

- **Il faut combattre la pauvreté.**
  It's necessary to / we must fight poverty.
- **Il faut combattre la famine dans le monde.**
  We should fight world famine.

- **Il faut condamner la violence.**
  It's necessary to condemn violence.
- **Il faut protéger les droits de l'homme.**
  It's necessary to protect human rights.
- **Il faut promouvoir l'égalité des chances.**
  We must promote equal opportunities.

The Verb 'Vouloir'

The verb **vouloir** means 'to want' and is followed by the infinitive form of a verb. You've already used it for expressing future plans (e.g. **Je veux devenir prof** – 'I want to become a teacher'), but it's also useful for inviting people out, and accepting or refusing invitations. Here's the verb **vouloir** in full:

Je veux	I want
Tu veux	You want
Il / Elle veut	He / She wants
Nous voulons	We want
Vous voulez	You want
Ils / Elles veulent	They want

Les manifestants veulent protester contre la discrimination. Tu veux aller à la manifestation avec moi?
The demonstrators want to protest against discrimination. Do you want to go to the demonstration with me?

Oui, je veux bien.
Yes, I'd love to (I want to).

Voulez-vous contribuer à une organisation caritative?
Do you want to contribute to a charity?

Non merci, je ne veux pas. Nous voulons faire du travail bénévole.
No thanks, I don't want to. We want to do some voluntary work.

Tackling Issues Affecting Society

aider	to help	**consacrer**	to devote, commit	**se plaindre**	to complain
il s'agit de…	it's about…	**déranger**	to disturb	**protéger**	to protect
agresser	to attack	**éviter**	to avoid	**protester**	to protest
battre	to beat	**garder**	to keep	**réaliser**	to achieve
se battre avec	to fight with	**lutter contre**	to struggle, fight against	**respecter**	to respect
cacher	to hide	**menacer**	to threaten		
combattre	to combat, fight	**plaindre**	to pity, feel sorry for		

Il ne faut pas cacher le problème.
We mustn't hide the problem.

Il faut lutter contre le racisme.
We must fight against racism.

Nous voulons éviter la guerre et garder la paix.
We want to avoid war and maintain peace.

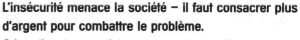

L'insécurité menace la société – il faut consacrer plus d'argent pour combattre le problème.
Crime threatens society – we must commit more money to fight this problem.

Je veux aider les sans-abris et j'ai l'intention de collecter de l'argent pour réaliser mon ambition.
I want to help the homeless and I intend to collect money to achieve my ambition.

The Pronoun 'On'

The pronoun **on** (literally 'one') is often used in French when you're not referring to a specific person. It can be translated as 'you', 'we' or 'they'. It's followed by the same form of the verb as **il** and **elle**. For example:

- **On proteste contre la guerre.**
  They're protesting against the war.

- **On dit que la violence devient pire.**
  They (people) say that violence is getting worse.
- **Si on veut combattre la pauvreté, on peut faire du travail bénévole pour aider les pauvres.**
  If you want to fight poverty, you can do voluntary work to help the poor.

Useful Expressions

- **On pourrait** we could, might
- **On devrait** we ought to, should

On pourrait aider les gens qui meurent de faim.
We could help people who are dying of hunger.

On devrait faire plus d'efforts pour combattre la famine.
We should make more effort to combat famine.

Quick Test

1 Say / write it in English:
   a) **Je veux protester contre l'insécurité.**
   b) **On devrait participer à la manifestation contre la guerre.**
   c) **Elle a l'intention de faire du travail bénévole pour une organisation caritative.**

2 Say / write it in French:
   a) He wants to protest against unemployment.
   b) I intend to achieve my ambitions.
   c) We should respect human rights.

Practice Questions

Reading

1 Choose one of the following adjectives to describe each of the people listed below.

généreuse   sévère   sportif   ennuyeux   gentille   intelligente   paresseux

a) Ma sœur a toujours de bonne notes à l'école. _____

b) Mon frère ne travaille pas à l'école et il ne fait jamais ses devoirs. _____

c) Ma mère me donne beaucoup d'argent de poche et elle m'achète des vêtements. _____

d) Mon père est très strict et il ne me permet pas de sortir avec mes amis. _____

2 In the passage below, Laura talks about her friends. Read the passage and answer the questions that follow in English.

> Ma meilleure amie s'appelle Alice. Elle a les cheveux longs et les yeux bleus. Elle est de taille moyenne, mais elle est plus grande que moi. Je m'entends bien avec elle parce que nous aimons le même genre de musique et nous faisons du shopping ensemble.
>
> Mon petit ami s'appelle Luc. Je sors avec lui depuis deux mois mais il m'énerve en ce moment parce qu'il veut rester tout le temps à la maison. Il ne veut pas aller au ciné, il n'aime pas le sport et il refuse d'aller aux magasins.

a) Describe Alice's appearance. Give three details.

     i) _____ **ii)** _____ **iii)** _____

b) Why does Laura get on with Alice? Give two details.

     i) _____ **ii)** _____

c) How long has Laura been going out with Luc? _____

d) Why isn't Laura happy with Luc at the moment? _____

Speaking

3 Give a full response to each of the questions below in French. Say your answer out loud.

     a) Comment t'appelles-tu?

     b) Quel âge as-tu?

     c) Comment es-tu physiquement?

     d) Comment est ta personnalité?

     e) **i)** Tu as des frères ou des sœurs?

           ii) Tu t'entends bien avec eux?

Writing

4 Imagine that you're the scriptwriter for a French soap opera. You need to write about a new character for the series. Write about each of the following in French.

a) The character's looks, personality and interests.

....

....

....

b) The character's family and friends and his / her relationships with others.

....

....

....

c) A storyline involving the new character.

....

....

....

5 You're writing about your plans for the future, including details about your ideal partner. Write about each of the following in French.

a) Your plans for the future and why.

....

....

....

b) Your ideal partner.

....

....

....

c) Your plans with regards to marriage and children.

....

....

Healthy and Unhealthy Lifestyles

Expressions with 'Avoir'

Some expressions in French use the verb **avoir** (to have) where we would use the verb 'to be' in English. For example:

- **J'ai faim** means 'I'm hungry'.
- **J'ai soif** means 'I'm thirsty'.

Other expressions that take **avoir** (rather than **être** as you might expect) include:

avoir chaud	to be hot
avoir froid	to be cold
avoir peur	to be frightened
avoir raison	to be right
avoir tort	to be wrong
avoir envie de	to feel like

Il mange beaucoup de fruits. Il a raison.
He eats a lot of fruit. He's right.

Je ne me sens pas bien. J'ai froid.
I don't feel well. I'm cold.

Tu as chaud? Enlève ton pull!
You're hot? Take off your jumper!

The Perfect Tense

The perfect tense is used in French to describe events that have happened and have a clear time limit, i.e. something that happened once and is over and done with. (Note that the imperfect tense is used for things that happened *more than* once or *used to* happen, or for interrupted actions.)

To form most verbs in the perfect tense you need to use the correct form of the present tense of **avoir**. Here it is in full:

J'ai	I have	**Nous avons**	We have
Tu as	You have	**Vous avez**	You have
Il / Elle a	He / She has	**Ils / Elles ont**	They have

You then follow **avoir** with part of the verb known as the past participle. For **-er** verbs, you form the past participle simply by taking off the **-er** and adding **-é**:

J'ai mangé	I ate, have eaten
Elle a travaillé	She worked, has worked
Nous avons acheté	We bought, have bought
Ils ont aidé	They helped, have helped

Note that the perfect tense means both 'I have done' something and 'I did' something. If the verb doesn't end in **-er**, you'll have to learn the past participle of the verb. Here are some common ones:

Infinitive	Meaning	Participle	Meaning
voir	to see	**vu**	saw
boire	to drink	**bu**	drank
dormir	to sleep	**dormi**	slept
recevoir	to receive	**reçu**	received
faire	to do / make	**fait**	did / made

Samedi dernier, j'ai joué au football.
Last Saturday, I played football.

J'ai commencé le travail à dix heures et j'ai fini à cinq heures.
I started work at 10 o'clock and I finished at 5.

J'ai mangé du poisson et j'ai bu du thé.
I ate fish and drank tea.

To make a perfect tense negative, put the negative **ne... pas** around **avoir**. For example:

- **Je n'ai pas dormi.**
  I didn't sleep.
- **Ils n'ont pas bu.**
  They didn't drink.

If you're forming a sentence using direct and indirect pronouns (e.g. me, you, him), the pronoun goes in front of **avoir**. For example:

- **Le patron m'a donné dix livres.**
  The boss gave me £10.
- **Je leur ai parlé pendant la journée.**
  I spoke to them during the day.

Healthy and Unhealthy Lifestyles

Time Expressions

généralement	generally	**sans cesse**	constantly, continuously
d'habitude	usually	**toujours**	always
normalement	normally	**encore**	still
la plupart du temps	most of the time	**encore une fois**	again
quelquefois / parfois	sometimes	**de nouveau**	again
de temps en temps	from time to time	**déjà**	already
rarement	rarely	**chaque**	each
tous les jours	every day	**chaque jour**	each / every day
tous les soirs	every evening	**chaque matin**	each / every morning

Je suis rarement malade.
I'm rarely ill.

Normalement, je dors bien.
Normally, I sleep well.

Je mange bien la plupart du temps.
I eat well most of the time.

An Active Lifestyle

Je me lève tôt et je fais de l'exercice.
I get up early and do some exercise.

Je promène le chien et je vais au travail à pied.
I walk the dog and I go to work on foot.

Je vais au gymnase tous les soirs.
I go to the gym every evening.

Je ne regarde jamais la télé et je me couche de bonne heure.
I never watch TV and I go to bed early.

An Inactive Lifestyle

Je fais la grasse matinée et je ne fais pas d'exercice.
I have a lie-in and don't do any exercise.

Je vais au travail en voiture.
I go to work by car.

Je ne vais jamais au gymnase.
I never go to the gym.

Je regarde la télé tous les soirs et je me couche très tard.
I watch TV every evening and go to bed very late.

Quick Test

1 Say / write it in English:
   a) **J'ai très chaud.**
   b) **J'ai joué au foot.**
   c) **Elles ont fait du shopping.**

2 Say / write it in French:
   a) She saw the match.
   b) He walks the dog every day.
   c) He goes to work by bus.

Healthy and Unhealthy Lifestyles

Smoking

Je fume des cigarettes.
I smoke cigarettes.

Je ne fume pas.
I don't smoke.

Je fume depuis deux ans.
I've been smoking for 2 years.

Je fume dix cigarettes par jour.
I smoke 10 cigarettes a day.

 Pourquoi?
Why?

Je le trouve relaxant.
I find it relaxing.

C'est sociable.
It's sociable.

Cela combat le stress.
It fights stress.

Cela aide à mincir.
It helps you lose weight.

NO SMOKING

 Pourquoi pas?
Why not?

Cela cause le cancer des poumons.
It causes lung cancer.

Le tabagisme passif est dangereux pour les non-fumeurs.
Passive smoking is dangerous for non-smokers.

Ça pue et les vêtements sentent mauvais.
It stinks and your clothes smell bad.

On a les dents et les doigts jaunes.
You get yellow teeth and fingers.

Negatives

The basic way to make a verb negative is to put **ne**… **pas** around the verb. For example:

- **Je ne sais pas.**
  I don't know.
- **Je ne comprends pas.**
  I don't understand.

Here are some more negative expressions:

ne… **rien**	nothing
ne… **jamais**	never
ne… **plus**	no / any longer
ne… **personne**	nobody

Je ne fume jamais.
I never smoke.

Ma mère ne fume plus.
My mother doesn't smoke anymore.

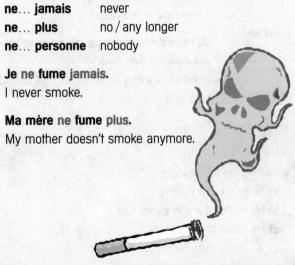

In the perfect tense, you have to make **avoir** negative (i.e. the negative expression 'wraps around' **avoir**). For example:

- **Je n'ai jamais fumé.**
  I've never smoked.
- **Il n'a jamais joué au tennis.**
  He's never played tennis.
- **Ils n'ont rien vu.**
  They saw nothing.
- **Elle n'a plus fait de ski.**
  She didn't ski anymore.

But note the exceptions **ne**… **personne** and **ne**… **que** (which means 'only'). When you use **ne**… **personne** or **ne**… **que**, the main verb (e.g. **vu**, **fume**) splits the expression. For example:

- **Je n'ai vu personne.**
  I didn't see anyone.
- **Il ne fume que deux cigarettes par jour.**
  He only smokes two cigarettes a day.

Note how **un, une, du, de la** and **des** change to **de** (or **d'**) after a negative expression. For example:

- **Je fume des cigarettes** ➡ **Je ne fume pas de cigarettes.**
  I smoke cigarettes. ➡ I don't smoke cigarettes.

Healthy and Unhealthy Lifestyles

Drugs

la drogue	drugs
accro	addicted
un(e) drogué(e)	a drug addict
la désintoxication	rehabilitation
consommer	to consume / take
se droguer	to take drugs
un toxicomane	an addict
la toxicomanie	addiction
un comprimé	tablet
une habitude	habit
une piqûre	injection
piquer	to inject
une drogue douce	soft drug
une drogue dure	hard drug
illicite	illegal
le cannabis	cannabis
la cocaïne	cocaine
l'ecstasy	ecstasy
l'héroïne	heroin
se passer de	to do without

La drogue est un gros problème.
Drugs are a big problem.

La drogue cause le crime.
Drugs lead to crime.

Les jeunes sont tentés par la drogue parce que c'est interdit.
Young people are tempted by drugs because they're illegal.

Ils croient que c'est cool de consommer de la drogue. Ils prennent de la drogue pour faire comme les autres.
They think it's cool to take drugs. They take drugs to be like others.

Ils se droguent à cause de la pression des pairs.
They take drugs because of peer pressure.

On ne connaît pas toutes les conséquences à long terme.
We don't know what the long-term consequences are.

More Negatives

Some more useful negatives are **nulle part** (nowhere) and **aucun / aucune** (none / no). For example:

- **Il n'est pas sportif. Il ne va jamais nulle part. Il aime mieux rester chez lui.**
  He's not sporty. He never goes anywhere. He prefers staying at home.
- **Aucun joueur n'a marqué de but. C'était un match nul ennuyeux.**
  No player scored a goal. It was a boring draw.

Some negatives can be used as the subject of a verb. For example:
- **Personne n'a gagné.** No-one won.

Quick Test

1. Say / write it in English:
   a) Il ne prend plus de drogue.
   b) Elle n'a que deux euros.
   c) Mon père n'a rien compris.

2. Say / write it in French:
   a) She no longer smokes.
   b) Drugs lead to violence.
   c) I never go anywhere.

Healthy and Unhealthy Lifestyles

Food

Here are some useful words for fruits and vegetables:

les fruits	fruits	**une orange**	orange		
un abricot	apricot	**un pamplemousse**	grapefruit		
un ananas	pineapple	**une pêche**	peach	**un chou**	cabbage
une banane	banana	**une poire**	pear	**un chou-fleur**	cauliflower
une cerise	cherry	**une pomme**	apple	**un concombre**	cucumber
un citron	lemon	**une prune**	plum	**des haricots verts**	green beans
une fraise	strawberry	**du raisin**	grapes	**des petits pois**	peas
une framboise	raspberry	**une tomate**	tomato	**une pomme de terre**	potato
un kiwi	kiwi fruit	**les légumes**	vegetables	**un radis**	radish
du melon	melon	**une carotte**	carrot	**une salade**	lettuce / salad

How to Say 'Some' and 'Any'

There are four different ways of saying 'some' or 'any' in French.

1. Masculine words take **du**. For example:
   - **Le chou** ➤ **Je voudrais du chou.**
     Cabbage ➤ I'd like some cabbage.
2. Feminine words take **de la**. For example:
   - **La salade** ➤ **Je veux de la salade.**
     Salad ➤ I want some salad.
3. Plural words take **des**. For example:
   - **Les fraises** ➤ **Je mange des fraises.**
     Strawberries ➤ I'm eating some strawberries
4. Words beginning with a vowel take **de l'**, whether the word is masculine or feminine. For example:
   - **L'ananas** ➤ **Je prends de l'ananas.**
     Pineapple ➤ I'm having some pineapple.

In questions, **du**, **de la**, **des** and **de l'** are often translated as 'any'. For example:
- **Avez-vous des petits pois?**
  Have you any peas?

N.B. The word **quelques** means 'some', in the sense of 'a few'. For example:
- **Quelques personnes aiment le chou.**
  Some / A few people like cabbage.

Drinks

du café	coffee
du chocolat	chocolate
du thé	tea
de l'eau	water
du coca	cola
de la limonade	lemonade
du jus d'orange	orange juice
de la bière	beer
du vin	wine
du cidre	cider

The verb **boire** (to drink) is irregular in French. Here it is in full:

Je bois	I drink, am drinking
Tu bois	You drink, are drinking
Il / Elle boit	He / She drinks, is drinking
Nous buvons	We drink, are drinking
Vous buvez	You drink, are drinking
Ils / Elles boivent	They drink, are drinking

Healthy and Unhealthy Lifestyles

At the Restaurant

la Carte — *the menu*

hors d'oeuvres — starters
entrées — starters

des crudités — raw vegetables
des fruits de mer — seafood
de la salade — salad
du saucisson — salami
du pâté — pâté
du jambon — ham
du potage — soup
de la soupe — soup

plats principaux — main courses
de la viande — meat
du poisson — fish
du poulet — chicken

la Carte — *the menu*

de l'agneau — lamb
du porc — pork
du steak — steak
une omelette — omelette
un oeuf — egg
des frites — chips

desserts — sweets/desserts
de la crème — cream
des glaces — ice cream
du fromage — cheese
de la tarte — tart
des gâteaux — cakes
de la pâtisserie — pastry

Qu'est-ce que vous prenez?
What are you having?

Qu'est-ce que vous voulez boire?
What do you want to drink?

Avez-vous choisi? Je recommande le porc.
Have you chosen? I recommend the pork.

L'addition, s'il vous plait.
The bill, please.

Quantities of Food and Drink

When you're giving quantities of food…
- **du** and **de la** change to **de**
- **de l'** changes to **d'**
- **des** changes to **de** (or **d'** before a vowel).

Un kilo de pommes et 500 grammes de fromage.
A kilo of apples and half a kilo of cheese.

Une bouteille d'eau et un morceau de gâteau.
A bottle of water and a piece of cake.

Un paquet de sucre et un pot de crème.
A packet of sugar and a pot of cream.

Quick Test

1. Say / write it in English:
   a) **Je voudrais des pommes de terre.**
   b) **Elle achète un kilo de poires.**
   c) **Il a choisi une glace à la fraise.**
2. Say / write it in French:
   a) I'd like some raspberries.
   b) She wants chicken and chips.
   c) He'd like a kilo of tomatoes.

Healthy and Unhealthy Lifestyles

Useful Verbs

boire	to drink
consommer	to consume
manger	to eat
éviter	to avoid
essayer	to try
prendre	to take, have
goûter	to taste

Les jeunes boivent trop d'alcool.
Young people drink too much alcohol.

J'évite de manger trop de chocolat.
I avoid eating too much chocolate.

Il ne faut pas consommer trop de graisse.
One shouldn't consume too much fat.

Elle ne prend jamais de viande rouge.
She never has red meat.

Nous essayons de manger équilibré.
We try to eat a balanced diet.

Alcohol

Je ne bois jamais, c'est dangereux pour le foie.
I never drink, it's dangerous for the liver.

Mon père boit de la bière avec modération.
My father drinks beer in moderation.

Il y a des jeunes qui boivent excessivement.
There are some young people who drink excessively.

On boit pour être sociable.
People drink to be sociable.

L'alcool provoque des accidents de la route.
Alcohol causes road accidents.

More Negatives

After negative expressions, you have to change **du**, **de la** and **des** to **de** (or **d'** before a vowel). For example:

- **Elle ne boit pas d'alcool.**
  She doesn't drink alcohol.
- **Ils ne mangent pas de choses sucrées.**
  They don't eat sweet things.
- **Je ne prends jamais de sucre.**
  I never take sugar.

The Pronoun 'En'

You'll often find the word **en** used in a sentence to mean 'of it' or 'of them'. We often don't bother to translate it into English. **En** goes before the verb, for example:

- **Avez-vous des pamplemousses? J'en prends deux.**
  Have you any grapefruits? I'll have two (of them).
- **Combien de tomates y a-t-il dans le frigo? Il y en a quatre.**
  How many tomatoes are there in the fridge? There are four (of them).

- **Le poisson est bon pour la santé. J'en mange une fois par semaine.**
  Fish is good for your health. I eat some (of it) once a week.

Healthy and Unhealthy Lifestyles

Healthy Diets

Il faut manger beaucoup de fruits et légumes et céréales.
You should eat a lot of fruit and vegetables and cereals.

Il faut boire beaucoup d'eau.
You should drink lots of water.

Il faut éviter trop de produits laitiers.
You should avoid too many dairy products.

Il ne faut pas consommer trop de graisse, sucre ou sel.
You shouldn't have too much fat, sugar or salt.

Adverbs

To form many adverbs, you simply take the feminine form of the adjective and add the ending **-ment**.

For example, the feminine form of **lent** (meaning 'slow') is **lente**. So the adverb is **lentement** (meaning 'slowly'). For example:

- **Il boit la bière très lentement.**
  He's drinking the beer very slowly.
- **Malheureusement, je mange beaucoup de bonbons.**
  Unfortunately, I eat a lot of sweets.
- **Ma sœur boit excessivement.**
  My sister drinks excessively.

Vraiment (meaning 'really' / 'truly') is an exception. It doesn't use the feminine form of **vrai**:

- **C'est vraiment délicieux.**
  It's really delicious.

Note also that the adverbs **vite** (quickly) and **soudain** (suddenly) don't obey this rule.

Recipes

une recette	a recipe
mettez	put
ajoutez	add
mélangez	mix
remuez	stir
versez	pour
faites cuire	cook

Pour faire une crêpe…
To make a pancake…

1. **Mettez de la farine et du lait dans un bol.**
   Put flour and milk into a bowl.
2. **Ajoutez deux oeufs et mélangez le tout.**
   Add two eggs and mix everything together.
3. **Versez un peu de pâte dans une poêle et faites cuire pendant une minute.**
   Pour a bit of the mixture into a frying pan and cook for one minute.
4. **Tournez la crêpe. Servez avec du sucre et de la confiture.**
   Turn the pancake over. Serve with sugar and jam.

(See p.56 for more on giving instructions.)

Quick Test

1. Say / write it in English:
   a) Je voudrais goûter des fruits de mer.
   b) Il mange des fruits tous les jours.
   c) Ma sœur ne prend jamais de légumes.

2. Say / write it in French:
   a) She eats very slowly.
   b) Have you any bananas?
   c) I'd like two of them.

Sports and Exercise

Sports

l'alpinisme	mountaineering	**le foot**	football	**le ping-pong**	table tennis
l'athlétisme	athletics	**le golf**	golf	**la planche à voile**	windsurfing
le basket	basketball	**la gymnastique**	gymnastics	**les promenades**	walks
courir	to run	**le handball**	handball	**les randonnées**	walks, hikes
la course	running	**la musculation**	bodybuilding	**le skate**	skateboarding
le cyclisme	cycling	**la natation**	swimming	**le ski nautique**	waterskiing
la danse	dance	**le patin à roulettes**	roller-skating	**les sports d'hiver**	winter sports
l'escalade	climbing	**patiner**	to skate	**le tennis**	tennis
l'équitation	horse-riding	**la pêche**	fishing		

Most of the words above take the verbs **aller** (to go),
faire (to do) and **jouer** (to play). For example:

- **J'aime jouer au basket.**
  I like playing basketball.
- **Je fais souvent de la gymnastique.**
  I often do gymnastics.
- **Ma sœur va à la pêche avec mon père.**
  My sister goes fishing with my father.
- **J'aime aller à la piscine. Je fais de la natation parce que c'est bon pour la santé.**
  I like going to the pool. I swim because it's good for your health.

Time Expressions

There are three different words to convey the length of
time spent on an activity. You have to decide exactly
what you want to say.

1 If you did something for a specific period of time but
you no longer do it, use **pendant** with the *perfect
tense*. For example:

- **J'ai joué au tennis pendant deux ans.**
  I played tennis for 2 years. (*and I don't anymore*)

2 If you're still doing the activity, use **depuis** with the
present tense. For example:

- **Je joue au golf depuis deux mois.**
  I've been playing golf for 2 months. (*and I still am*)

3 If you haven't yet done something, use **pour** with the
future tense. For example:

- **Je vais faire du ski pour une semaine.**
  I'm going skiing for a week. (*but I haven't yet started*)

The Present Participle

To form the present participle, take the **nous** form of the
present tense, remove the **-ons** and add **-ant**.

When it's used after the preposition **en**, the present
participle means 'in', 'on', 'by' or 'while'. For example:

- **Je fais du jogging en écoutant de la musique.**
  I jog while listening to music.
- **En arrivant au gymnase, il a fait des exercices.**
  On arriving at the gym, he did some exercise.

Saying When You're Doing an Activity

Venir de, **être en train de** and **être sur le point de** are expressions you can use to be specific about when you have done, are doing or will do an activity.

You use **venir de** in the present tense to convey that you've just done something. For example:

- **Je viens de jouer au rugby.**
  I've just played rugby.
- **Tu viens de finir?**
  Have you just finished?
- **Il / Elle vient de faire de la voile.**
  He / She has just been sailing.
- **Nous venons de gagner le match.**
  We've just won the match.
- **Vous venez de me battre.**
  You've just beaten me.
- **Ils / Elles viennent de perdre le jeu.**
  They've just lost the game.

You use **être en train de** for when you're in the middle of doing something. For example:

- **Il est en train de faire du vélo.**
  He's just out cycling.
- **Ils ne peuvent pas vous voir. Ils sont en train de manger.**
  They can't see you. They're in the middle of eating.

You use **être sur le point de** for something you're about to do. For example:

- **Je suis sur le point de partir pour le stade.**
  I'm about to set off for the stadium.
- **Ils sont sur le point de marquer un but.**
  They're about to score a goal.

Useful Words

une équipe	a team
un but	a goal
gagner	to win
perdre	to lose
participer	to take part
adhérer à	to join
un match nul	a draw
une victoire	a win
une défaite	a loss

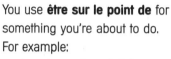

Le sport est relaxant et on se sent mieux.
Sport is relaxing and you feel better.

C'est bon pour le cœur et cela aide à perdre du poids.
It's good for the heart and it helps you to lose weight.

C'est sociable. On se fait de nouveaux amis.
It's sociable. You make new friends.

Quick Test

1. Say / write it in English:
   a) **Je joue au foot une fois par semaine.**
   b) **Je viens de jouer au squash.**
   c) **Je suis sur le point d'aller au centre sportif.**
2. Say / write it in French:
   a) I've been playing hockey for three years.
   b) He's going to Paris for three days.
   c) While playing football, he scored a goal.

Practice Questions

Reading

1 The following statements are reasons for and against smoking. Put each statement into the correct column in the table.

Pour	Contre

A C'est relaxant.

B Ça cause le cancer.

C Le tabagisme passif est très dangereux pour les non-fumeurs.

D Les vêtements sentent mauvais.

E On a les dents jaunes.

F C'est agréable quand on est avec ses amis.

G C'est un bon remède contre le stress.

2 Read what these people say about their eating habits and then answer the questions that follow.

Au petit déjeuner je prends des céréales et généralement je bois du chocolat chaud. A midi, je rentre à la maison et je prends le déjeuner avec maman et ma petite sœur. Le soir, pour le dîner, je mange de la viande ou du poisson avec des légumes.

Morgane

Je ne prends jamais de petit déjeuner. À midi je mange à la cantine scolaire. Je prends souvent une salade et un yaourt. Le soir, je dine vers sept heures et demie avec mes parents. Je ne mange jamais de viande ni de poisson.

Annie

Pour le petit déjeuner, je prends généralement du pain grillé avec de la confiture et un jus d'orange. Je prends le petit déjeuner dans la cuisine à sept heures. A l'heure du déjeuner, j'aime manger à la cantine au collège. Je préfère le steak-frites. Le soir, je ne mange pas beaucoup. On dine vers huit heures.

Philippe

a) Who doesn't have breakfast? ....

b) Who has fruit juice at breakfast time? ....

c) Who drinks hot chocolate? ....

d) Who could be a vegetarian? ....

e) Who goes home for lunch? ....

f) Who eats at 8pm? ....

Speaking

3 Give a full response to each of the questions below in French. Say your answer out loud.

a) Qu'est-ce que tu aimes manger?

b) Est-ce que tu fumes? Pourquoi / pourquoi pas?

c) Tu bois souvent de l'alcool?

d) Que fais-tu pour garder la forme?

e) Tu aimes faire du sport?

Writing

4 Write an account about your lifestyle. Write about each of the following in French.

a) Say what exercise you do and what you've done recently to keep fit.

....

....

....

b) Talk about what you like to eat and drink, and why.

....

....

....

c) Give some details about what you intend to do in the future to stay healthy.

....

....

....

....

5 Write about what you did at the weekend. Write about each of the following in French.

a) Say what you did at home last weekend.

....

....

....

b) Say what you had to eat and drink.

....

....

....

c) Say what you did outside the house.

....

....

....

Free Time Activities

Leisure and Pastimes

Qu'est-ce que tu fais pour les loisirs? Quel est ton passe-temps?

What do you do for leisure? What are your pastimes?

Here are some useful phrases to say what you do when you go out.

Je… I…		
	vais au cinéma	go to the cinema
	vais aux concerts	go to concerts
	danse	dance
	sors	go out
	vais en boite	go clubbing
	vais au match	go to a match
	vais au théâtre	go to the theatre
	vais à la pêche	go fishing

Here are some useful phrases to say what you do when you stay in.

Je… / J'… I…		
	surfe sur Internet	surf the net
	joue aux jeux-vidéo	play computer games
	lis	read
	regarde la télé	watch TV
	regarde des DVD	watch DVDs
	joue du piano	play the piano
	joue de la guitare	play the guitar
	chante	sing
	écoute de la musique	listen to music
	écris	write
	envoie des e-mails	send emails

The Perfect Tense with 'Être'

A small number of very common verbs use the verb **être** to form the perfect tense, instead of **avoir**. You still need to add the past participle in order to form the full perfect tense. For example:

- **Je suis allé au parc d'attractions.**
  I went to the theme park.

The past participle has a masculine and a feminine form. The past participle has to agree with the gender of the pronoun (i.e. **je**, **vous**, **il**, **elle**, people's names, etc.). For example:

- **Pascal est allé au cinéma, mais sa sœur Nicole est allée au théâtre.**
  Pascal went to the cinema, but his sister Nicole went to the theatre.

Here is the perfect tense of the verb **aller** in full:

Je suis allé / allée	I went
Tu es allé / allée	You went
Il est allé	He went
Elle est allée	She went
Nous sommes allés / allées	We went
Vous êtes allé / allés / allée / allées	You went
Ils sont allés	They went
Elles sont allées	They went

The following verbs are all formed in the same way:

Infinitive	Meaning	Past Participle
sortir	to go out	**sorti**
rester	to stay	**resté**
arriver	to arrive	**arrivé**
partir	to leave	**parti**
entrer	to enter	**entré**
monter	to go up	**monté**
descendre	to go down	**descendu**
venir	to come	**venu**
naitre	to be born	**né**
mourir	to die	**mort**
tomber	to fall	**tombé**
retourner	to return	**retourné**
rentrer	to come home	**rentré**
devenir	to become	**devenu**

As with verbs that take **avoir**, negatives are formed by wrapping **ne… pas** around the correct form of **être**. For example:

- **Je ne suis pas allé au concert.**
  I didn't go to the concert.

At the Cinema

un film d'amour	a romance film	une comédie musicale	a musical
un film à suspense	a suspense film	un drame	a drama
un polar	a detective film	un film historique	a historical film
un western	a western	un film de science-fiction	a science-fiction film
un film d'horreur	a horror film		
un film d'épouvante	a scary film	un dessin animé	a cartoon
une comédie	a comedy		

Talking About Films

Je préfère les films comiques parce que j'aime bien rire avec mes amis. Je n'aime pas tellement les films de science-fiction, je les trouve barbants et sans intérêt.

I prefer comic films because I like a good laugh with my friends. I don't like science-fiction films very much, I find them boring and uninteresting.

Récemment, j'ai vu un film français excellent qui s'appelle *Les Choristes*.

Recently I saw an excellent French film called *Les Choristes*.

Il s'agit d'un groupe d'élèves difficiles dans un internat dans les années 40. Un surveillant décide de créer une chorale. La musique transforme la vie de ses élèves.

It's about a group of difficult pupils in a boarding school in the 1940s. A supervisor decides to start a choir. Music transforms the lives of his pupils.

C'est un film touchant et amusant.

It's a touching and funny film.

The Verb 'Venir'

Besides being one of the irregular verbs that takes **être** in the perfect tense, **venir** (to come) is also irregular in the present tense. Here it is in full:

Je viens	I come
Tu viens	You come
Il / Elle vient	He / She comes
Nous venons	We come
Vous venez	You come
Ils / Elles viennent	They come

The expression **venir de** is very useful because it can be used to express the idea of just having done something. For example:

- **Elle vient de voir ce film.**
  She's just seen this film.
- **Je viens de manger du pop-corn.**
  I've just eaten some popcorn.

Quick Test

1 Say / write it in English:
   a) **Je suis sorti avec mes copains.**
   b) **Elle n'aime pas du tout les films d'épouvante.**
   c) **Ils ont chanté dans une chorale.**

2 Say / write it in French:
   a) I'd like to see a romantic film.
   b) He went home late.
   c) They saw the film then went to the cafe.

Free Time Activities

Asking Someone Out

Here are some useful phrases for asking people to go out with you.

Tu veux…?	Do you want…?	**Tu veux aller au cinéma avec moi?**	**Tu peux venir au concert?**
Tu as envie de…?	Do you feel like…?	Do you want to go to the cinema with me?	Can you come to the concert?
Tu peux…?	Can you…?		**Ça te dit de faire une promenade à la campagne?**
Ça te dit de…?	Do you fancy…?	**Tu as envie de jouer au badminton?**	
		Do you feel like playing badminton?	Do you fancy a walk in the country?

Accepting an Invitation

Oui, je veux bien	Yes, I'd like that	**Pourquoi pas?**	Why not?	**On se retrouve devant le cinéma à sept heures, d'accord?**	
Certainement	Certainly	**On se retrouve où? Et à quelle heure?**		We'll meet in front of the cinema at 7, OK?	
Avec plaisir	With pleasure	Where shall we meet? And what time?			
D'accord	OK				

Refusing an Invitation

Je ne peux pas	I can't	**Je dois me laver les cheveux.**	**Je dois rendre visite à mes grands-parents.**	
Je ne veux pas	I don't want to	I must wash my hair.		
Certainement pas!	Certainly not!	**Je dois finir mes devoirs.**	I have to visit my grandparents.	
Non, merci	No thanks	I must finish my homework.		
Fiche-moi la paix!	Get lost!			

Possessive Pronouns

The possessive pronouns are 'mine', 'yours', 'his', 'hers', 'ours' and 'theirs'.

These words have a masculine singular form, a feminine singular form, a masculine plural form and a feminine plural form. Note that 'ours', 'yours' and 'theirs' only have one plural form (for masculine *and* feminine):

Mine	**le mien, la mienne, les miens, les miennes**
Yours (singular)	**le tien, la tienne, les tiens, les tiennes**
His / Hers	**le sien, la sienne, les siens, les siennes**
Ours	**le nôtre, la nôtre, les nôtres**
Yours (plural or polite)	**le vôtre, la vôtre, les vôtres**
Theirs	**le leur, la leur, les leurs**

C'est à qui, ce livre?
Whose book is this?

C'est le mien.
It's mine.

C'est à qui, cette veste?
Whose jacket is this?

C'est la mienne.
It's mine.

In informal conversation, you can often convey the same idea by using the pronouns **moi, toi, lui, elle, nous, vous, eux** and **elles**. For example:

- **C'est à moi.**
  It's mine.

Free Time Activities

Reading

la lecture	reading
un livre	a book
un roman	a novel
un magazine / une revue	a magazine
une bande dessinée (une BD)	a cartoon
un article	an article
le courrier du cœur	a problem page

Je passe beaucoup de temps à lire.
I spend a lot of time reading.

J'apprécie surtout les romans historiques et les bandes dessinées.
I especially appreciate historical novels and cartoons.

Je lis des magazines parce que je m'intéresse aux articles sur la mode.
I read magazines because I'm interested in the articles on fashion.

Playing Musical Instruments

Note that **jouer** à is used for games and sports. For example:

- **Je joue au Scrabble.**
  I play Scrabble.

But, for musical instruments, you have to use **jouer de**. For example:

- **Je joue du piano depuis deux ans.**
  I've been playing the piano for two years.
- **Mon ami aime jouer de la flûte.**
  My friend likes playing the flute.

Here are some useful words for talking about which musical instruments you play.

le violon	violin	**la batterie**	drums
la guitare	guitar	**le clavier**	keyboard
la trompette	trumpet	**la clarinette**	clarinet
la flûte	flute	**le saxophone**	saxophone
le piano	piano	**le hautbois**	oboe

Listening to Music

J'aime la musique de toutes sortes mais surtout le jazz.
I like all kinds of music, but especially jazz.

Je ne peux pas supporter le rap – je le trouve monotone.
I can't stand rap music – I find it monotonous.

Mon chanteur favori est... parce qu'il a une belle voix et j'aime les paroles de ses chansons.
My favourite singer is… because he has a lovely voice and I like the words of his songs.

Je vais souvent à des concerts parce que j'aime l'ambiance.
I often go to concerts because I like the atmosphere.

J'ai toujours mon baladeur iPod sur moi, c'est tellement pratique.
I always have my iPod with me, it's so practical.

Quick Test

1. Say / write it in English:
   a) **Tu veux manger au restaurant?**
   b) **Il vient d'apprendre à jouer du piano.**
   c) **C'est à qui, ce manteau?**

2. Say / write it in French:
   a) Do you want to play football?
   b) Whose is that house?
   c) It's theirs, but I don't like the garden.

Shopping, Money, Fashion and Trends

Shopping

une bijouterie	jewellers	**un hypermarché**	hypermarket	**une quincaillerie**	hardware shop
une boucherie	butchers	**une laiterie**	dairy	**le rayon**	food department
une boulangerie	bakers	**un marchand**	greengrocers	**alimentation**	
une charcuterie	delicatessen	**de légumes**		**un supermarché**	supermarket
une confiserie	sweet shop	**le marché**	market	**un magasin**	clothes shop
une épicerie	grocers	**une parfumerie**	perfume shop	**de vêtements**	
un grand	department	**une pâtisserie**	cake shop		
magasin	store	**une poissonnerie**	fishmongers		

Irregular Adjectives

Most adjectives form their feminine form by adding **-e**. These are regular adjectives. For example:

- un **chou vert**   a green cabbage
- une **pomme verte**   a green apple

There are also many irregular adjectives:

Adjectives ending in **-f** change to **-ve** in the feminine form. For example:

- un **magasin neuf**   a new shop
- une **épicerie neuve**   a new grocers

Adjectives ending in **-x** change to **-se** in the feminine form. For example:

- Il **est heureux**   He is happy
- Elle **est heureuse**   She is happy

Adjectives ending in **-n** often double the **n** and add **-e** in the feminine form. For example:

- Le **restaurant est moyen.**
  The restaurant is average.
- Elle **est de taille moyenne.**
  She is of average height.

Note these other irregular adjectives:

Frais (cool, fresh) ➡ **fraîche**:
- le **fromage frais**   fresh cheese
- de l'eau **fraîche**   fresh water

Sec (dry) ➡ **sèche**:
- un **vin sec**   a dry wine
- une **pomme sèche**   a dry apple

Blanc (white) ➡ **blanche**:
- un **vin blanc**   a white wine
- la **viande blanche**   white meat

Long (long) ➡ **longue**:
- un **voyage long**   a long journey
- une **visite longue**   a long visit

At the Shops

Je peux vous aider? Vous désirez?
Can I help you? What would you like?

Je cherche le rayon des vêtements hommes.
I'm looking for the men's department.

C'est au troisième étage / au sous-sol / rez-de-chaussée.
It's on the third floor / in the basement / on the ground floor.

L'escalier roulant ne marche pas. Où est l'ascenseur?
The escalator isn't working. Where's the lift?

Où est la caisse? Où sont les soldes?
Where's the till? Where are the sales?

Je veux me plaindre. Je voudrais un remboursement.
I want to complain. I'd like a refund.

Shopping, Money, Fashion and Trends

'This', 'That', 'These' and 'Those'

To say 'this', 'that' and 'these' in French, you use **ce**, **cette** and **ces**.

In front of a masculine word use **ce**:
- **Ce magasin est ouvert.**   This shop is open.

In front of a feminine word use **cette**:
- **Cette pomme est délicieuse.** This apple is delicious.

In front of a plural word use **ces**, whether it's masculine or feminine:
- **Ces magasins sont fermés.**   These shops are closed.

- **Ces pommes sont vieilles.**   Those apples are old.

For masculine words beginning with a vowel or silent h, there's a special form of **ce**:
- **Cet oeuf est dur.**
  This egg is hard.
- **Cet homme cherche de l'eau minérale.**
  That man's looking for mineral water.

If you need to distinguish between 'this' and 'that', you can add **-ci** (this) or **-là** (that) to the end of the word. For example:
- **Ce magasin-ci est ouvert, mais ce magasin-là est fermé.**
  This shop's open, but that shop's closed.

Useful Verbs

accepter	to accept	**trouver**	to find
acheter	to buy	**ouvrir**	to open
chercher	to look for	**payer**	to pay for
choisir	to choose	**quitter**	to leave
commander	to order	**signer**	to sign
essayer	to try on	**vendre**	to sell
fermer	to close		

Buying Things

Le prix est bon?	Is it a good price?	**en hausse / en baisse**	up / down
C'est combien?	How much is it?	**une augmentation**	an increase
Ça fait combien?	How much does it come to?	**la monnaie**	change
une offre spéciale	a special offer	**un billet (de banque)**	bank note
une réduction	a reduction	**une pièce de monnaie**	coin
des rabais	reductions	**des livres sterling**	(British) pounds sterling
cher / pas cher	expensive / cheap	**un portefeuille**	wallet
bon marché	cheap	**un porte-monnaie**	purse
élevé / bas	high / low		

Quick Test

1. Say / write it in English:
   a) **Je voudrais payer avec cette carte de crédit.**
   b) **Elle cherche un T-shirt au marché.**
   c) **Ce magasin est trop grand.**

2. Say / write it in French:
   a) This lift isn't working.
   b) She prefers these strawberries.
   c) The wine is very expensive.

Shopping, Money, Fashion and Trends

Clothes

un blouson	jacket	**un imperméable**	raincoat	**un pull**	jumper
une casquette	cap	**un jean**	jeans	**une robe**	dress
un chapeau	hat	**une jupe**	skirt	**un sac à main**	handbag
des chaussettes	socks	**un jogging**	tracksuit	**un short**	shorts
des chaussures	shoes	**un maillot de bain**	bathing suit	**un sweat-shirt**	sweatshirt
une chemise	shirt	**un manteau**	coat	**un T-shirt**	T-shirt
un costume	suit	**une montre**	watch	**une veste**	jacket
une cravate	tie	**un pantalon**	trousers		

Je cherche une chemise en coton.
I'm looking for a cotton shirt.

Vous faites quelle taille?
What size are you?

Je cherche des baskets.
I'm looking for trainers.

Vous faites quelle pointure?
What size are you?

Je peux l'essayer / les essayer?
Can I try it / them on?

Où est la cabine d'essayage?
Where are the changing rooms?

Avez-vous la même chemise en bleu?
Have you got the same shirt in blue?

Je regrette, il n'y en a plus.
I'm sorry, we haven't got any more.

Describing Clothes

en coton	(made of) cotton	**uni**	plain	
en cuir	(made of) leather	**à rayures**	with stripes, stripy	
en soie	(made of) silk			
en laine	(made of) wool	**à pois**	with spots, spotted	
en jean	(made of) denim			
en polyester	(made of) polyester	**à carreaux**	checked	
en velours	(made of) velvet	**large**	baggy	
écossais	tartan	**court**	short	
étroit	tight	**long**	long	

Le pantalon en cuir ne lui va pas.
The leather trousers don't suit him.

Je n'aime pas porter des chemises en polyester quand il fait chaud.
I don't like wearing polyester shirts when it's hot.

Cette cravate-ci à pois est plus chère que cette cravate-là à rayures.
This spotted tie is more expensive than that stripy tie.

Asking 'Which One?'

Masculine singular:
Il y a beaucoup de pulls. Lequel préfères-tu?
There are lots of jumpers. Which one do you prefer?

Feminine singular:
Il y a un grand choix de robes. Lequelle préfères-tu?
There's a big choice of dresses. Which one do you prefer?

Masculine plural:
Je n'aime pas ces T-shirts. Lesquels?
I don't like those T-shirts. Which ones?

Feminine plural:
J'ai choisi des chaussettes. Lesquelles?
I've chosen some socks. Which ones?

Shopping, Money, Fashion and Trends

'This One', 'That One', 'These Ones'

Masculine singular:

Ce pull	This jumper
Celui-ci	This one
Celui-là	That one

Feminine singular:

Cette veste	This jacket
Celle-ci	This one
Celle-là	That one

Masculine plural:

Ces chapeaux	These hats
Ceux-ci	These (ones)
Ceux-là	Those (ones)

Feminine plural:

Ces chaussures	These shoes
Celles-ci	These (ones)
Celles-là	Those (ones)

Describing Your Style

Elle aime le look gothique. Elle porte des vêtements sombres et des bottes noires.
She likes the goth look. She wears dark clothes and black boots.

Il aime mieux le look rappeur. Il porte un T-shirt large et un pantalon trop long avec des baskets blancs.
He prefers the rapper look. He wears a baggy T-shirt and trousers that are too long with white trainers.

Pour aller en vacances elle va acheter…
To go on holiday, she's going to buy…

Pour assister au mariage de sa sœur, elle va mettre…
To attend her sister's wedding, she's going to wear…

The Verb 'Mettre'

The verb **mettre** (to put / to put on) is irregular. Here it is in full:

Je mets	I put, am putting (on)
Tu mets	You put, are putting (on)
Il / Elle met	He / She puts, is putting (on)
Nous mettons	We put, are putting (on)
Vous mettez	You put, are putting (on)
Ils / Elles mettent	They put, are putting (on)

Je mets mon nouveau blouson.
I'm putting on my new jacket.

Elle met un pantalon parce qu'elle n'aime pas porter des jupes.
She's putting on trousers because she doesn't like wearing skirts.

The past participle of the verb **mettre** is **mis**. For example:

* **Ils ont mis leurs meilleurs vêtements.**
  They've put on their best clothes.

Note that the verb **se mettre à** means 'to start'. For example:

* **Il se met à travailler plus dur.**
  He's starting to work harder.

Quick Test

1 Say / write it in English:
   a) **Je mets une chemise blanche.**
   b) **Elle n'aime pas la veste en jean.**
   c) **Elle préfère celle-là en laine.**

2 Say / write it in French:
   a) This skirt is too tight.
   b) She prefers these white ones.
   c) That jumper is too expensive.

New Technology

Watching Television

une émission	programme	**une série**	series	**Je n'aime pas regarder la télé. Il y a trop de feuilletons et de télé-réalité.**
le petit écran	small screen	**une série policière**	detective programme	I don't like watching TV. There are too many soaps and reality TV programmes.
les informations	news	**la publicité**	adverts	
les actualités	news	**un jeu**	game show	
la météo	weather forecast	**une chaine**	TV channel	**Je regarde la télé tous les jours. J'aime surtout les informations et les documentaires sur les animaux.**
un documentaire	documentary	**la télé par satellite**	satellite TV	I watch TV every day. I particularly like the news and documentaries on animals.
une émission pour les enfants	children's programme	**la télé par câble**	cable TV	
		haute définition	HD (high definition)	
un dessin animé	cartoon			
une émission sportive	sports programme	**un écran plat**	flat screen	**Je trouve qu'il y a trop de publicité à la télé.**
		numérique	digital	I think there's too much advertising on TV.
une émission musicale	music programme	**enregistreur à disque dur**	hard disc recorder	
un feuilleton	soap	**un lecteur DVD**	DVD player	

Useful Verbs

Je / J'… I…	**appelle**	call	**enregistre**	record	**surfe**	surf
	téléphone à	phone	**télécharge**	download	**envoie**	send
	regarde	watch	**éteins**	switch off	**bavarde**	chat
	écoute	listen to	**allume**	switch on		

Relative Pronouns

Qui and **que** are relative pronouns, meaning 'which' or 'who'. For example:

- **J'ai un nouveau portable qui a un appareil cinq megapixels.**
  I have a new phone, which has a 5-megapixel camera.

- **C'est le portable que ses parents lui ont offert.**
  That's the phone that his parents gave him.

In the previous sentences, **qui** and **que** both replace the word 'phone'. But, when you want to replace a whole sentence or clause, you need to use **ce qui** or **ce que** instead. For example:

- **J'ai un portable prépayé, ce qui est plus pratique pour moi.**
  I have a pay-as-you-go phone, which is more practical for me.

- **Les appels de l'étranger sont très chers, ce que je trouve inacceptable.**
  Calls from abroad are very expensive, which I find unacceptable.

In the sentences above, **ce qui** and **ce que** replace the clauses 'I have a pay-as-you-go phone' and 'Calls from abroad are very expensive'.

See p.61 for more on **qui** and **que**.

Mobile Phones

mon téléphone portable	my mobile phone
un texto	text
téléphone prépayé	pre-paid
téléphone avec forfait	contract
un appareil	camera
une carte mémoire	SIM card
internet haut débit	broadband
une facture	a bill
une sonnerie	ring tone
un lecteur MP3 / baladeur MP3	MP3 player
gratuit	free
le GPS	sat-nav
équipé de…	equipped with…

Je ne peux pas vivre sans mon portable, mais à la fin du mois la facture est très chère.
I can't live without my mobile, but at the end of the month the bill is very expensive.

Les portables sont utiles pour la sécurité mais dans un train les gens qui parlent au téléphone sont vraiment agaçants.
Mobiles are useful for safety, but people who talk on the phone on trains are really annoying.

On dit que les portables sont dangereux pour le cerveau.
People say that mobile phones are dangerous for the brain.

MP3 Players

une gamme	a range
un écran tactile	touch screen
le poids	the weight
une pile	battery
le logiciel	software
la mémoire	memory

Mon baladeur MP3 n'a pas beaucoup de mémoire et je dois recharger les piles tous les jours.
My MP3 player hasn't got much memory and I have to recharge the batteries every day.

Ma sœur a un lecteur MP3 qui est très léger avec un écran tactile. Elle peut facilement télécharger des vidéoclips gratuitement.
My sister has an MP3 player that is very light and has a touch screen. She can download videos easily for free.

Impersonal Verbs

You've already met the verb **falloir** (to be necessary), which is only ever used in the **il** form: **il faut**.

Another useful impersonal verb is **valoir** (to be worth). For example:
- **Il vaut choisir un téléphone prépayé.**
  It's worth choosing a pre-paid phone.

Il vaut mieux means 'It's worthwhile'. For example:
- **Il vaut mieux envoyer des textos, c'est moins cher.**
  It's worthwhile sending texts, it's less expensive.

Quick Test

1. Say / write it in English:
   a) J'apprécie les feuilletons.
   b) Elle a acheté un nouveau portable.
   c) Elles envoient souvent des textos.

2. Say / write it in French:
   a) I would like an MP3 player.
   b) I download music, which is easy.
   c) His ring tone is annoying.

New Technology

Computers and the Internet

un ordinateur	computer
un ordinateur portable	laptop
le logiciel	software
une imprimante	printer
un clavier	keyboard
une souris	mouse
une cartouche	ink cartridge
un disque compact	CD
une clé USB	USB memory stick
un courriel	email message
l'e-mail	email
une adresse	address
un lien	link
un forum	newsgroup
la toile	the web
un site	site
cliquer	to click
le serveur	server
tchatcher	to chat
un blog	blog

Je passe beaucoup de temps sur mon ordinateur. J'envoie des e-mail, je télécharge des vidéoclips et je joue aux jeux.
I spend a lot of time on my computer. I send emails, download videos and play games.

Je surfe sur Internet pour trouver des renseignements pour m'aider avec mes devoirs.
I surf the Internet to find information to help me with my homework.

Pour moi, le réseau social est indispensable.
For me, social networking is indispensable.

On peut acheter des choses à des prix très bas, bien que la fraude soit un gros problème.
You can buy things at low prices, although fraud is a big problem.

Les enfants peuvent rencontrer des gens malhonnêtes à moins qu'ils ne soient surveillés.
Children can meet dishonest people unless they're supervised.

The Subjunctive

After certain expressions, such as **bien que** (although), **pour que** (so that), **pourvu que** (provided that) and **à moins que** (unless), you have to use a special form of the verb known as the subjunctive.

You have no need to use it for GCSE, but you may come across it in reading and listening texts. Here's the verb **être** in the subjunctive:

Je sois	I am
Tu sois	You are
Il / Elle soit	He / She is
Nous soyons	We are
Vous soyez	You are
Ils / Elles soient	They are

Mon ordinateur marche bien qu'il soit vieux.
My computer works, although it's old.

-er verbs are the same in the subjunctive except for the **nous** and **vous** forms, which are the same as the imperfect:

- **Je travaille pour que je puisse acheter un nouveau portable.**
  I work so that I can buy a new phone.

- **Il peut surfer sur Internet pourvu qu'il finisse ses devoirs.**
  He can surf the net provided that he finishes his homework.

Other common irregular subjunctive verbs are:
- **je fasse (faire)**
- **j'aie (avoir)**
- **j'aille (aller)**
- **je puisse (pouvoir).**

Adverts

un spot publicitaire	a TV advert
les petites annonces	classified ads
une page de publicité	radio advert, commercial break
vanter	to boast
encourager	to encourage
exagérer	to exaggerate
mentir	to lie
une vedette	a star / celebrity
destiné à	aimed at
le / la meilleur(e)	the best
un slogan	slogan
la cible	the target (audience)

La publicité est mauvaise parce qu'elle encourage les gens à acheter les choses dont ils n'ont pas besoin.
Advertising is bad because it encourages people to buy things that they don't need.

La publicité est utile parce qu'elle donne des renseignements aux consommateurs.
Advertising is useful because it gives consumers information.

La publicité exploite les enfants quand elle vante et exagère les qualités des produits.
Advertising exploits children when it boasts about and exaggerates the quality of products.

The Superlative

As you've seen already, to make comparisons you use **plus** or **moins** with an adjective. For example:

* **La publicité est plus amusante que certaines émissions.**
  Advertising is funnier than some programmes.
* **Les vedettes sont moins efficaces que les animaux dans la publicité.**
  Celebrities are less effective than animals in adverts.

Plus means 'more' and **moins** means 'less'. But, if you use **le**, **la** or **les** before **plus** or **moins**, they mean 'most' and 'least'. For example:

* **Mon portable est le plus chic.**
  My phone's the most smart / smartest.
* **C'est le village le moins connu de la France.**
  It's the least well-known village in France.

Le meilleur / la meilleure / les meilleurs / les meilleures are used to say 'the best'. For example:

* **Le meilleur vin du monde.**
  The best wine in the world.

The French for 'the worst' is **le pire / la pire** or **les pires**. For example:

* **C'est le pire slogan dans l'histoire de la publicité.**
  It's the worst slogan in advertising history.

Quick Test

1. Say / write it in English:
   a) **Je surfe souvent sur Internet.**
   b) **Il achète des livres sur des sites français.**
   c) **Il télécharge de la musique bien que ce soit illégal.**

2. Say / write it in French:
   a) I hate adverts for cars.
   b) My sister has the best computer.
   c) Although it's new, the computer is slow.

Holidays

Countries Around the World

When you're talking about going to different countries, there are different ways to say 'to' or 'in', depending on whether the country is masculine, feminine or plural.

Masculine countries take **au**. For example:
- **Montréal se trouve au Canada.**
  Montreal is (situated) in Canada.

Feminine countries take **en**. For example:
- **Nous allons en France.**
  We're going to France.

Plural countries take **aux**. For example:
- **Je rêve d'aller aux États-Unis.**
  I dream of going to the United States.

Islands tend to take **à**. For example:
- **Je vais aller à Malte.**
  I'm going to go to Malta.

Most countries are feminine:

L'Allemagne	Germany	**La Grande-**	Great
L'Angleterre	England	**Bretagne**	Britain
L'Australie	Australia	**La Grèce**	Greece
L'Autriche	Austria	**L'Inde**	India
La Belgique	Belgium	**L'Irlande**	Ireland
La Chine	China	**L'Italie**	Italy
L'Ecosse	Scotland	**La Russie**	Russia
L'Espagne	Spain	**La Suisse**	Switzerland
La France	France		

But, watch out for these masculine ones:

Le Canada	Canada	**Le Pays**	Wales
Le Danemark	Denmark	**de Galles**	
Le Japon	Japan	**Le Portugal**	Portugal
Le Pakistan	Pakistan		

Nationalities

A common mistake is to say the French word for the nationality rather than the country. Make sure you don't confuse the names of countries with the words used to describe the people who live there:

Allemand(e)	German	**Français(e)**	French	**Canadien(ne)**	Canadian
Anglais(e)	English	**Britannique**	British	**Danois(e)**	Danish
Australien(ne)	Australian	**Grec (Grecque)**	Greek	**Japonais(e)**	Japanese
Autrichien(ne)	Austrian	**Indien(ne)**	Indian	**Pakistanais(e)**	Pakistani
Belge	Belgian	**Irlandais(e)**	Irish	**Gallois(e)**	Welsh
Chinois(e)	Chinese	**Italien(ne)**	Italian	**Hollandais(e)**	Dutch
Ecossais(e)	Scottish	**Russe**	Russian	**Portugais(e)**	Portuguese
Espagnol(e)	Spanish	**Suisse**	Swiss		

Where to Stay on Holiday

à la campagne	to / at the country	**dans une caravane**	in a caravan
au bord de la mer	to / at the seaside	**dans une auberge de jeunesse**	in a youth hostel
à la montagne	to / at the mountains	**dans un gîte**	in a cottage
en ville	to / in a city	**dans une villa**	in a villa
dans un hôtel	in a hotel	**dans un appartement**	in an apartment
dans un camping	on a campsite		

Getting to Your Destination

en autobus	by bus	**en avion**	by plane
en car	by coach	**en tramway**	by tram
en taxi	by taxi	**à pied**	on foot
en voiture /		**à vélo**	by bike
auto	by car	**à moto**	by motorbike
en bateau	by boat	**à cheval**	by horse
en croisière	on a cruise	**par le train**	by train

Je n'aime pas voyager en car.
Le voyage est long et fatigant.
I don't like travelling by coach.
The journey is long and tiring.

Je préfère voyager en avion,
parce que c'est plus rapide.
I prefer travelling by plane
because it's quicker.

Useful Verbs

Here are some useful verbs for saying what you do
on holiday.

Je / J'…
I…

bronze	sunbathe
me repose	rest
nage	swim
visite	visit
fais du lèche-vitrine	window-shop
fais de l'auto-stop	hitchhike
fais de la voile	sail
fais de la planche à voile	windsurf
pars	set off
voyage	travel
accompagne	accompany
achète	buy
loue	hire / rent
écris	write
oublie	forget

Tous les ans, nous partons en France où mes parents
louent un gîte à la campagne.
Every year we go to France where my parents rent a
cottage in the country.

En vacances, j'oublie tout. Je bronze
à la plage, je nage dans la mer et je
visite les monuments historiques.
On holiday, I forget everything. I
sunbathe on the beach, swim in the
sea and visit historic monuments.

Cette année, en février, je pars dans
les Alpes avec mon école pour faire
des sports d'hiver. J'adore le ski.
This year in February, I'm setting off to
the Alps with my school to do winter
sports. I love skiing.

The Pronoun 'Y'

The pronoun **y** means 'there' and is very useful, but
remember that it goes before the verb. For example:

* **J'adore l'Espagne. J'y vais tous les ans.**
  I love Spain. I go there every year.
* **Nous allons en Grèce cet été. Nous y allons en avion.**
  We're going to Greece this summer. We're getting
  there by plane.

Quick Test

1. Say / write it in English:
   a) **Je vais au bord de la mer.**
   b) **Il va toujours en Inde.**
   c) **Elle aime la cuisine espagnole.**
2. Say / write it in French:
   a) I want to go sailing.
   b) She doesn't like going to Wales.
   c) The girls are Dutch.

Holidays

Describing Your Holiday

Vous êtes parti en vacances cet été?
Did you go on holiday this summer?

Où? Quand? Avec qui? Et comment?
Where? When? Who with? And how?

Je suis parti en Bretagne en France.
I went to Brittany in France.

J'y ai passé quinze jours au mois de juillet.
I spent 2 weeks there in July.

J'y suis allée avec mes copains.
I went with my friends.

Nous avons pris le bateau.
We took the boat.

Saying 'Before' and 'After'

To say 'before' is easy in French. Use **avant** (before) plus **de**, plus the infinitive. For example:

- **avant de manger**
  before eating
- **avant de partir**
  before setting off

To say 'after' is a little more complicated. Use **après** (after) plus **avoir** or **être**, plus the past participle. For example:

- **après avoir mangé**
  after eating
- **après être parti**
  after setting off

Après avoir nagé, j'ai bronzé près de la piscine.
After swimming, I sunbathed beside the pool.

Après être arrivées, les filles sont allées à l'hôtel.
After arriving, the girls went to the hotel.

Note that agreements are needed for **être** verbs. Reflexive verbs all take **être** and need the extra pronoun. For example:

- **Après m'être levé, j'ai pris le petit déjeuner.**
  After getting up, I had breakfast.
- **Après s'être douchée, elle s'est habillée.**
  After having a shower, she got dressed.

Useful Prepositions

là-bas	over there	**sauf**	except
dedans	inside	**selon**	according to
dehors	outside	**par**	by, through
en bas	downstairs	**vers**	towards, about (with time)
en haut	upstairs		
près de	near	**au bout de**	at the end of
loin de	a long way from	**au fond de**	at the back of
contre	against	**autour de**	around

Où est le bateau? C'est là-bas.
Where's the boat? It's over there.

On peut jouer au minigolf tous les jours sauf le dimanche.
You can play crazy golf every day except Sunday.

J'aime manger dehors quand il fait chaud.
I like eating outside when it's hot.

Il a mangé vers huit heures.
He ate at about 8.

Getting Around

la route	road	**le port**	port	**la sortie**	exit
l'autoroute	motorway	**le pont**	deck, bridge	**la sortie de secours**	emergency exit
en panne	breakdown	**la douane**	customs	**poussez**	push
un bouchon	a jam, hold-up	**l'aéroport**	airport	**tirez**	pull
des travaux	roadworks	**un retard**	delay	**départ**	departure
la station-service	petrol station	**le billet**	ticket	**arrivée**	arrival
la gare	station	**le passeport**	passport	**à l'heure**	on time
le guichet	ticket office	**l'assurances**	insurance (policy)	**en avance**	early
le quai	platform	**l'entrée**	entrance	**en retard**	late

Next Year's Holiday

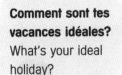
Comment sont tes vacances idéales?
What's your ideal holiday?

Je voudrais partir aux États-Unis.
I'd like to go to the USA.

Je veux y passer un mois.
I want to spend a month there.

J'irai avec mes copains parce que c'est plus amusant et j'aurai plus de liberté.
I'll go with my friends because it's more enjoyable and I'll have more freedom.

Nous voyagerons en avion et logerons dans un grand hôtel de luxe.
We'll travel by plane and stay in a big, luxurious hotel.

J'ai envie de faire du shopping dans les grands magasins à New York.
I want to go shopping in the department stores in New York.

Lengths of Time

The French for 'a week' is **une semaine** or **huit jours** ('8 days'). The French for 'two weeks' is **deux semaines** or **quinze jours** ('15 days'). The French for 'a fortnight' is **une quinzaine**.

With dates, **à partir de** means 'from' and **jusqu'à** means 'until'. For example:

- **Je vais restir en France** à partir du **deux** jusqu'au **dix août.**
  I'm going to stay in France from the 2nd to the 10th of August.

Di	3	10	17	24	31
Lu	4	11	18	25	
Ma	5	12	19	26	
Me	6	13	20	27	
Je	7	14	21	28	
Ve	18	15	22	29	
Sa	29	16	23	30	

Quick Test

1. Say / write it in English:
   a) Je vais en Italie pour huit jours.
   b) Avant d'arriver, j'ai mangé un sandwich.
   c) Après avoir mangé, j'ai bu un café.
2. Say / write it in French:
   a) I want to stay until the 9th of July.
   b) The boys are late.
   c) They intend to leave at about 4.

Holidays

Useful Words

le logement	accommodation	un grand lit	double bed
l'accueil	reception	une nuit	a night
un ascenseur	lift	la note	the bill
la baignoire	bath	le premier étage	first floor
un balcon	balcony	le rez-de-chaussée	ground floor
une chambre	a bedroom	le robinet	tap
une douche	shower	la salle de bains	bathroom
une clef	key	un sèche-cheveux	hair dryer
le drap	sheet	du savon	soap
un escalier	stairs	une serviette	towel
un lavabo	wash basin	une vue	a view
un lit	bed		

Organising Accommodation

Je voudrais réserver une chambre pour deux nuits.
I'd like to reserve a room for 2 nights.

Je veux une chambre avec douche et une vue sur la mer.
I want a room with a shower and a sea view.

J'ai réservé une chambre pour deux personnes au nom de…
I've booked a room for two people in the name of…

A quelle heure est le petit déjeuner? C'est compris?
What time is breakfast? Is it included?

La télé dans notre chambre ne marche pas et il n'y a pas de serviettes dans la salle de bains.
The TV in our room doesn't work and there are no towels in the bathroom.

Pouvez-vous me réveiller à sept heures demain matin?
Can you wake me at 7 tomorrow morning?

J'ai perdu ma clef, je suis désolé.
I've lost my key, I'm sorry.

Asking Questions

After a question word (an interrogative), you often invert the verb (i.e. change its position) as in the English 'How are you?', rather than 'How you are?'.

But this sometimes gets tricky in French. Questions like 'What time is breakfast?' or 'Where is my room?' are easy: **À quelle heure est le petit déjeuner? Où est ma chambre?** But look at this example:
- What time does Marie get up?
  A quelle heure Marie se lève-t-elle?

You can avoid this tricky inversion by using **est-ce que**. This keeps the normal word order. So the question becomes:
- **A quelle heure est-ce que Marie se lève?**
  What time does Marie get up?

Other examples include:
- **Quand est-ce que vous partez?**
  When are you leaving?
- **Pourquoi est-ce que vous êtes arrivés en retard?**
  Why did you arrive late?

Camping

le bloc sanitaire	wash room
eau potable	drinking water
l'emplacement	pitch
le gaz	gas
une machine à laver	washing machine
des plats à emporter	takeaway food
une poubelle	bin
un sac de couchage	sleeping bag
la salle de jeux	games room
la tente	tent

Avez-vous de la place pour une caravane? C'est combien par nuit?
Have you space for a caravan? How much is it per night?

On peut louer des vélos?
Can we hire bikes?

Le terrain est inondé. Il n'y a pas d'électricité.
The ground is flooded. There's no electricity.

Il n'y a pas d'eau chaude. Les douches sont froides.
There's no hot water. The showers are cold.

Holiday Problems

J'ai perdu…	I've lost…
On m'a volé…	I've had… stolen
Je l'ai laissé(e)…	I left it…
C'était…	It was…

le bureau des objets trouvés	lost property
mon appareil (photo)	my camera
mon portefeuille	my wallet
mon porte-monnaie	my purse
mon sac à main	my handbag
mon parapluie	my umbrella

un accident de la route	road accident
un pneu crevé	flat tyre
tomber en panne	to break down
heurter	to collide, to hit
renverser	to knock down
blessé	hurt, injured
un piéton	pedestrian
un conducteur	driver
un camion	lorry, truck

J'ai perdu mon portefeuille hier dans la rue. C'est en cuir noir, et il y avait cinquante euros dedans.
I lost my wallet yesterday in the street. It's made of black leather and it had 50 euros inside.

J'ai vu un accident ce matin. Une voiture a heurté un vélo et le cycliste est tombé. Le conducteur n'était pas blessé mais le cycliste s'est cassé la jambe.
I saw an accident this morning. A car hit a bike and the cyclist fell off. The driver wasn't hurt but the cyclist broke his leg.

On m'a volé mon sac et je n'ai plus d'argent parce que ma carte de crédit était dedans.
I've had my bag stolen and I haven't got any more money because my credit card was inside the bag.

Quick Test

1. Say / write it in English:
   a) **Une chambre pour une personne.**
   b) **Je voudrais rester deux nuits.**
   c) **Le piéton est blessé.**

2. Say / write it in French:
   a) **I want to stay for four nights.**
   b) **She has lost her purse.**
   c) **The view is superb.**

Weather

The Weather

une averse	shower	ensoleillé	sunny	un orage	thunderstorm
le brouillard	fog	beau	fine	orageux	stormy, thundery
la brume	mist	mauvais	bad	la pluie	rain
la chaleur	heat	froid	cold	sec	dry
chaud	hot	la glace	ice	le soleil	sun
le ciel	sky	humide	damp	la température	temperature
le climat	climate	la météo	forecast	une tempête	storm
couvert	cloudy	mouillé	wet	le temps	weather
un degré	degree	la neige	snow	le tonnerre	thunder
doux	mild	un nuage	cloud	trempé	soaked
un éclair	lightning	nuageux	cloudy	le vent	wind
une éclaircie	sunny period	l'ombre	shade		

Useful Verbs

Le soleil brille	The sun's shining	Il fait beau	It's fine
Il gèle	It's freezing	Il fait froid	It's cold
Il neige	It's snowing	Il fait du vent	It's windy
Il pleut	It's raining		

The Weather Forecast

Demain, il fera beau dans le nord. Il y aura de belles éclaircies, mais dans l'ouest il fera du vent et il y aura des averses.
Tomorrow, it'll be fine in the north. There will be some lovely sunny spells, but in the west it'll be windy with showers.

Dans l'est, il fera assez froid avec un risque de pluie. Dans le sud, il fera très chaud mais il y aura des orages le soir.
In the east it'll be quite cold with the risk of rain. In the south it'll be very hot, but there will be thunderstorms in the evening.

La température maximale sera de 25 degrés.
The maximum temperature will be 25 degrees.

Describing What the Weather was Like

To say what the weather was like, you normally use the imperfect tense (explained on p.65). For example:

- **Il pleuvait.**
  It was raining.
- **Il faisait beau.**
  It was fine.
- **Il y avait de la neige.**
  There was snow.
- **Le soleil brillait.**
  The sun was shining.

If you want to refer to a specific, limited time then you need to use the perfect tense. For example:

- **Hier soir, il y a eu un orage.**
  Last night, there was a storm.
- **Il a fait du brouillard ce matin.**
  It was foggy this morning.
- **Il a plu pendant une heure.**
  It rained for an hour.

The Future Tense

In order to form the future tense, most verbs (e.g. **finir**, 'to finish') use the infinitive and add the following endings:

Je finirai	I'll finish
Tu finiras	You'll finish
Il / Elle finira	He / She will finish
Nous finirons	We'll finish
Vous finirez	You'll finish
Ils / Elles finiront	They'll finish

If the verb ends in **-e**, take this off before forming the future tense. For example:

- **Boire** ➡ **Je boir**ai
- **Vendre** ➡ **Tu vendr**as
- **Prendre** ➡ **Il prendr**a

Some verbs need to be learned separately, but they all take the same endings:

Être ➡	**Je serai** (I'll be)
Avoir ➡	**J'aurai** (I'll have)
Aller ➡	**J'irai** (I'll go)
Faire ➡	**Je ferai** (I'll do / make)
Voir ➡	**Je verrai** (I'll see)
Venir ➡	**Je viendrai** (I'll come)
Devenir ➡	**Je deviendrai** (I'll become)
Recevoir ➡	**Je recevrai** (I'll receive)
Pouvoir ➡	**Je pourrai** (I'll be able to)
Devoir ➡	**Je devrai** (I'll have to)
Vouloir ➡	**Je voudrai** (I'll like)
Savoir ➡	**Je saurai** (I'll know)
Tenir ➡	**Je tiendrai** (I'll hold)
Obtenir ➡	**J'obtiendrai** (I'll obtain)

Je finirai mes devoirs ce soir.
I'll finish my homework tonight.

Il deviendra fermier.
He'll become a farmer.

Il fera beau.
It will be fine (weather).

Ils seront tous les deux professeurs.
They'll both be teachers.

Il y aura du brouillard le matin et plus tard il fera plus chaud, mais il pleuvra le soir. Il y aura un risque de verglas sur les routes.
There will be fog in the morning and later it'll be warmer, but it will rain in the evening. There will be a risk of black ice on the roads.

Be careful with sentences containing **quand** (when) or **dès que** (as soon as). Although they translate into English as 'When I am' or 'As soon as I am', they're formed in French using the future tense. For example:

- **Quand je serai plus grande, j'irai à l'université.**
  When I'm older I'll go to university.
- **Quand elle aura dix-huit ans, elle apprendra à conduire.**
  When she's 18, she'll learn to drive.
- **Dès qu'il quittera l'école, il prendra une année sabbatique.**
  As soon as he leaves school, he'll take a gap year.

Remember, there are ways of avoiding the future tense, such as the use of future indicators (e.g. **je vais**, **je voudrais**, **je veux**) followed by the infinitive.

Quick Test

1 Say / write it in English:
   a) **Il fait du soleil.**
   b) **Il fera chaud.**
   c) **Lundi, il a fait mauvais.**

2 Say / write it in French:
   a) It is windy and cold.
   b) She likes the sun.
   c) It will be foggy.

Getting Around

Useful Words

un aéroport	airport	**une carte**	map	**le parking**	car park
un arrêt de bus	bus stop	**une moto**	motorbike	**un piéton**	pedestrian
un automobiliste	motorist	**un train**	train	**une station**	underground station
un avion	plane	**un tramway**	tram	**une station-service**	petrol station
un autobus	bus	**une voiture / auto**	car	**un vol**	flight

Asking for and Giving Directions

Pardon, madame	Excuse me, madam	**Prenez la première à gauche**	Take the first left
Excusez-moi, monsieur	Excuse me, sir	**Prenez la deuxième à droite**	Take the second right
Pour aller au centre-ville?	How do I get to the town centre?		
Il y a une banque près d'ici?	Is there a bank near here?	**Traversez la rue / le pont**	Cross the street / bridge
		Allez jusqu'aux feux	Go to the traffic lights
Où est la cathédrale?	Where's the cathedral?	**C'est sur votre droite**	It's on your right
Où est le café le plus proche?	Where's the nearest café?	**Au coin de la rue**	At the corner of the street
		Au carrefour	At the crossroads
Tournez à gauche / droite	Turn left / right	**Au rond-point**	At the roundabout
Continuez tout droit	Go straight on	**Quittez l'autoroute**	Leave the motorway

Giving Instructions

To give instructions and orders, you need to use a form of the verb known as the imperative.

If you're addressing a person with **tu**, use the **tu** form of the present tense of the verb, but without **tu**. You must also take off the **-s** of **-er** verbs. For example:

- **Mange tes légumes!** Eat your greens!
- **Prends la première à droite.** Take the first on the right.
- **Continue tout droit.** Go straight on.
- **Traverse le pont.** Cross the bridge.

If you're addressing a person / people with **vous**, use the **vous** form of the present tense, but without the **vous**. For example:

- **Mangez bien!** Eat well!
- **Prenez l'argent.** Take the money.
- **Continuez à travailler.** Carry on working.
- **Traversez l'autoroute.** Cross the motorway.

Using the **nous** form of the present tense without the **nous** means 'let's' do something. For example:

- **Jouons au tennis.** Let's play tennis.
- **Allons au ciné.** Let's go to the cinema.

Travelling by Car

l'essence	petrol	**le péage**	toll booth	**le volant**	steering wheel
le gazole	diesel	**le permis de conduire**	driving licence	**Les freins ne marchent pas.**	
les freins	brakes	**le pneu (crevé)**	(flat) tyre	The brakes aren't working.	
le feu rouge	red light	**la roue**	wheel		
le moteur	engine	**stationner**	to park	**Ma voiture est tombée en panne sur l'A6.**	
le pare-brise	windscreen	**tomber en panne**	to break down	My car has broken down on the A6.	

Travelling by Train

la gare	(train) station	**les renseignements**	information	**composter**	to cancel a ticket
l'entrée	entrance	**un horaire**	timetable	**une valise**	suitcase
la sortie	exit	**le guichet**	ticket office	**des bagages**	luggage
la sortie de secours	emergency exit	**un billet**	ticket	**la consigne**	left luggage
		un billet simple	single ticket	**la salle d'attente**	waiting room
arrivées	arrivals	**un aller-retour**	return ticket	**le quai**	platform
départs	departures	**un carnet**	book of 10 tickets		

Buying a Ticket and Getting Information

Je voudrais un aller simple pour Paris.
I'd like a single ticket to Paris.

Je voudrais voyager en deuxième classe.
I'd like to travel second class.

Je veux réserver une place.
I want to reserve a seat.

A quelle heure part le prochain train pour Nice?
What time does the next train for Nice leave?

Le train part de quel quai?
Which platform does the train leave from?

A quelle heure arrive le train?
What time does the train arrive?

C'est direct ou est-ce qu'il faut changer?
Is it direct or do I have to change?

On peut prendre la correspondance à Lyon.
You can change in Lyon.

Avez-vous un horaire, s'il vous plaît?
Have you got a timetable, please?

Travelling by Bus

Quel bus va au centre-ville? C'est quelle ligne?
Which bus goes to the town centre? What number is it?

Où est l'arrêt le plus proche?
Where's the nearest bus stop?

Un ticket, c'est combien?
How much is the bus ticket?

Useful Verbs

voyager	to travel
monter dans…	to get on
descendre de…	to get off
attendre	to wait
prendre la correspondence	to change
arriver	to arrive
partir	to set off
s'asseoir	to sit down
rester debout	to stand

Quick Test

1. Say / write it in English:
   a) Continuez tout droit et tournez à gauche aux feux.
   b) Où est le restaurant le plus proche?
2. Say / write it in French:
   a) How do I get to the beach?
   b) What time does the train arrive?

Practice Questions

Reading

1 Choose the correct country from the options given to match each description below.

la France   **l'Italie**   **l'Espagne**   **les États-Unis**   **l'Allemagne**   **l'Angleterre**

a) C'est un grand pays européen. La capitale est Paris. _____

b) Ici on mange des pizzas et des pâtes. La capitale est Rome. _____

c) C'est un grand pays puissant. La capitale est Washington. _____

d) Le climat est chaud et beau. La capitale est Madrid. _____

e) Il pleut beaucoup et on mange du poisson-frites. La capitale est Londres. _____

f) Ici on mange des saucisses et on boit de la bière. La capitale est Berlin. _____

2 In the passage below, Isabelle talks about her holiday. Read the passage and answer the questions that follow in English.

> Il y a deux ans, je suis allée dans les Alpes pour faire du ski. Je suis partie en février et j'ai passé une semaine dans les Alpes françaises. J'ai voyagé en car. C'était long et fatigant. Je suis restée dans un petit hôtel. Pendant le journée, j'ai fait du ski ou j'ai fait des promenades. Le soir, je suis allée dans un bar où j'ai bu du chocolat. Il a fait très froid et il a beaucoup neigé.

a) Where did Isabelle go on holiday? _____

b) Why did she go there? _____

c) How long did she stay? _____

d) How did she get there? _____

e) What was her opinion of the journey? _____

f) Where did she stay? _____

g) What did she do in the evenings? _____

h) What was the weather like? _____

Speaking

3 Give a full response to each of the questions below in French. Say your answer out loud.

a) Qu'est-ce que tu aimes faire en vacances?

b) Où es-tu allé(e) en vacances l'année dernière?

c) Qu'est-ce que tu as fait?

d) Quel temps a-t-il fait?

Writing

4 Write an account of a holiday you have been on. Write about each of the following in French.

a) Where you went and how you got there.

....

....

....

b) Where you stayed and what you did during your visit.

....

....

....

c) Where you'd like to go next year and why.

....

....

....

....

5 Write about your plans for a day out, for example, at the seaside. Write about each of the following in French.

a) How you're going to get there.

....

....

....

b) What you're hoping to do during the day and why.

....

....

....

c) What happened the last time you went there.

....

....

....

Home and Local Area

Describing Your House

au premier étage	upstairs / first floor	**une cuisine**	kitchen	**la véranda**	conservatory
au rez-de-chaussée	downstairs / ground floor	**le grenier**	attic, loft	**le garage**	garage
		une pièce	room	**le jardin**	garden
chez moi	at my house	**un salon**	lounge	**un arbre**	tree
un bureau	study	**la salle à manger**	dining room	**une fleur**	flower
une cave	cellar	**une salle de séjour**	living room	**le gazon**	grass
une chambre	bedroom	**la salle de bains**	bathroom	**la pelouse**	lawn
		le WC	toilet	**le hangar**	shed

Dans ma maison, il y a quatre pièces au rez-de-chaussée: le salon, la cuisine, la salle à manger et le bureau.
In my house there are 4 rooms downstairs: the lounge, the kitchen, the dining room and the study.

Au premier étage, il y a trois chambres, le WC et une salle de bains.
Upstairs there are 3 bedrooms, the toilet and a bathroom.

Il y a un petit jardin devant la maison et un grand jardin derrière.
There's a small garden in front of the house and a large garden behind.

Le garage est à côté de la maison.
The garage is next to the house.

The Verb 'Faire'

Many activities in the house can be described using the verb **faire** (to do / make). Here it is in full:

Je fais	I do, am doing
Tu fais	You do, are doing
Il / Elle fait	He / She does, is doing
Nous faisons	We do, are doing
Vous faites	You do, are doing
Ils / Elles font	They do, are doing

Faire is used in a lot of expressions that are to do with jobs around the house. For example:

faire la cuisine	to do the cooking
faire les courses	to go shopping
faire le jardinage	to do the gardening
faire la lessive	to do the washing
faire le lit	to make the bed
faire le ménage	to do the housework
faire le repassage	to do the ironing
faire la vaisselle	to do the washing-up

Qu'est-ce que tu fais pour aider à la maison?
What do you do to help at home?

Ma sœur lave la voiture. Mon frère fait le repassage.
My sister washes the car. My brother does the ironing.

J'aime faire la cuisine, mais je déteste faire mon lit.
I like doing the cooking, but I hate making my bed.

Mes parents font le jardinage.
My parents do the gardening.

Useful Verbs

laver	to wash	**passer l'aspirateur**	to do the vacuuming	**ranger**	to tidy
débarrasser la table	to clear the table	**promener le chien**	to walk the dog	**nettoyer**	to clean
mettre la table	to set the table	**sortir la poubelle**	to put the bin out		

How Often?

These expressions of time are helpful when saying how often you do something:

rarement	rarely	une fois par semaine	once a week	**Je promène le chien deux fois par semaine.**
ne… jamais	never			I walk the dog twice a week.
souvent	often	deux fois par semaine	twice a week	**Je fais souvent la vaisselle, mais je ne range jamais ma chambre.**
tous les jours	every day			
quelquefois	sometimes	régulièrement	regularly	I often do the washing-up, but I never tidy my room.
de temps en temps	from time to time	généralement	usually	
		d'habitude	usually	

Using 'Qui', 'Que' and 'Dont'

Qui is used to say 'who' or 'which' when there's a verb immediately after it. For example:

* **J'ai ma propre chambre qui est très grande.**
  I have my own room, which is very large.
* **C'est mon père qui fait la cuisine chez nous.**
  It's my dad who does the cooking in our house.

Que is used to say 'which' or 'whom' when there's a pronoun immediately after it. For example:

* **J'ai une grande chambre que j'adore.**
  I have a large bedroom, which I love.
* **Ma mère est une personne que je respecte beaucoup.**
  My mother is a person whom I respect greatly.

Dont is used to say 'whose'. For example:

* **C'est la dame dont la fille est jolie.**
  It's the lady whose daughter is pretty.
* **Voici la famille dont la maison est grande.**
  There's the family whose house is big.

The Verb 'Devoir'

The verb **devoir** means 'to have to' or 'must'. Here it is in full:

Je dois	I must, have to
Tu dois	You must, have to
Il / Elle doit	He / She must, has to
Nous devons	We must, have to
Vous devez	You must, have to
Ils / Elles doivent	They must, have to

Qu'est-ce que tu dois faire?
What do you have to do?

Je dois ranger ma chambre. Ma sœur doit sortir la poubelle. Mes frères doivent faire la vaisselle.
I must tidy my room. My sister must put the bin out. My brothers must do the washing-up.

Quick Test

1. Say / write it in English:
   a) **J'aime la cuisine qui est moderne.**
   b) **Mon frère doit nettoyer sa chambre.**
   c) **Mes parents font souvent le jardinage. Le jardin est très beau.**
2. Say / write it in French:
   a) My sister hates doing the housework.
   b) Downstairs, there's a large lounge and a kitchen.
   c) I like vacuuming but I rarely do the ironing.

Home and Local Area

What's in Your House?

une armoire	wardrobe	**un fauteuil**	armchair	**un miroir**	mirror
une bibliothèque	bookcase	**une fenêtre**	window	**une moquette**	carpet
un canapé	sofa	**un four à**	microwave	**un mur**	wall
une chaise	chair	**micro-ondes**		**un ordinateur**	computer
le chauffage	central heating	**un frigo**	fridge	**un placard**	cupboard
central		**un lavabo**	basin	**le plancher**	floor
une cuisinière	cooker	**un lave-vaisselle**	dishwasher	**le plafond**	ceiling
une douche	shower	**un lit**	bed	**une porte**	door
un escalier	stairs	**une machine**	washing machine	**un réveil**	alarm clock
une étagère	shelf	**à laver**		**un rideau**	curtain
un évier	sink	**les meubles**	furniture	**un tapis**	carpet, rug

Describing Your Room

Dans ma chambre, il y a un lit, une armoire et une chaise.
In my room, there's a bed, a wardrobe and a chair.

Je partage ma chambre avec ma sœur.
I share my room with my sister.

J'ai un ordinateur et une télé dans ma chambre.
I have a computer and a TV in my room.

Les murs sont bleus et les rideaux jaunes.
The walls are blue and the curtains are yellow.

J'ai ma propre chambre. Elle est très confortable.
I have my own room. It's very comfortable.

Saying Where Things Are

The following words are called prepositions. They're used to describe where something is.

dans	in
sur	on
sous	under
devant	in front of
derrière	behind
entre	between
à côté de	next to
en face de	opposite
au coin de	in the corner of
à gauche de	to the left of

Il y a deux fauteuils dans le salon.
There are two armchairs in the lounge.

La cuisine est à côté de la salle à manger.
The kitchen is next to the dining room.

Le jardin est derrière la maison.
The garden is behind the house.

L'armoire est entre la fenêtre et le lit.
The wardrobe is between the window and the bed.

Le chat est sur le lit.
The cat is on the bed.

Be careful if the word after **à côté de** or **en face de** is masculine. Instead of '**de le**', use **du**. For example:

- **La petite table est à côté du lit.**
  The little table is next to the bed.
- **Ma maison est en face du garage.**
  My house is opposite the garage.
- **Au coin du salon, nous avons une bibliothèque.**
  In the corner of the lounge we have a bookcase.

Daily Routine

These verbs will help you to talk about your routine at home.

se lever	to get up
se réveiller	to wake up
se laver	to have a wash
se doucher	to have a shower
se brosser	to brush
s'habiller	to get dressed
prendre le petit déjeuner	to have breakfast
quitter la maison	to leave the house
rentrer	to come home
faire la grasse matinée	to have a lie-in
se coucher	to go to bed

A quelle heure est-ce que tu te lèves?
What time do you get up?

Je me réveille à sept heures du matin.
I wake up at 7 o'clock in the morning.

Je me lève tout de suite.
I get up straightaway.

Je me lave dans la salle de bains et je me brosse les cheveux.
I have a wash in the bathroom and I brush my hair.

Je m'habille dans ma chambre.
I get dressed in my room.

Je prends le petit déjeuner à huit heures et je quitte la maison à huit heures vingt.
I have breakfast at 8 o'clock and I leave the house at 8.20.

Le week-end, je fais la grasse matinée.
At the weekend I have a lie-in.

A quelle heure est-ce que tu te couches?
What time do you go to bed?

Je me couche à dix heures et demie.
I go to bed at 10.30.

Where is Your House?

Ma maison se trouve…	My house is situated…
au centre-ville	in the town centre
en banlieue	in the suburbs
à la campagne	in the country
au bord de la mer	at the seaside
à la montagne	in the mountains
près de la ville	near town
dans un village	in a village
loin de la mer	a long way from the sea

C'est…	It is…
une maison individuelle	a detached house
une maison jumelée	a semi-detached house
un appartement	a flat
une ferme	a farm
une villa	a villa

Ma maison est près des magasins, c'est pratique.
My house is near the shops, it's practical.

Le centre-ville est loin de ma maison. Ce n'est pas très commode.
The town centre is a long way from my house. It's not very convenient.

Quick Test

1. Say / write it in English:
    a) Le salon est entre la cuisine et le bureau.
    b) La moquette est verte et rouge.
    c) Le chien est sous le lit.
2. Say / write it in French:
    a) My house is situated in the suburbs.
    b) I get up at 7.30am every day.
    c) I have breakfast in the kitchen.

Home and Local Area

Your Local Area

Ma ville se trouve…	My town is….
• **dans le nord / le sud**	in the north / south
• **dans l'est / l'ouest**	in the east / west
• **au centre**	in the centre
…**de l'Angleterre / de la France**	…of England / France
Au centre-ville, il y a…	In the town centre, there is…
• **une banque**	a bank
• **beaucoup de circulation**	a lot of traffic
• **une bibliothèque**	a library
• **un centre commercial**	a shopping centre
• **un centre sportif**	a sports centre
• **un château**	a castle
• **une église**	a church

• **des embouteillages**	traffic jams
• **une gare routière**	a bus station
• **un hôtel de ville**	a town hall
• **un marché**	a market
• **un musée**	a museum
• **un office de tourisme**	a tourist information office
• **une piscine**	a swimming pool
• **une plage**	a beach
• **une zone piétonne**	a pedestrian zone
C'est…	It's…
• **une ville industrielle**	an industrial town
• **une ville touristique**	a tourist town
• **une ville commerciale**	a commercial town
• **une ville historique**	an historical town

The Verb 'Pouvoir'

The verb **pouvoir** means 'to be able' ('can'). It's very useful when talking about what there is to do in your area. Here it is in full:

Je peux	I'm able, I can
Tu peux	You're able, you can
Il / Elle peut	He / She is able, he / she can
Nous pouvons	We're able, we can
Vous pouvez	You're able, you can
Ils / Elles peuvent	They're able, they can

On peut, meaning 'one / you can', is particularly useful. For example:

• **On peut visiter des monuments historiques.**
You can visit historical monuments.
• **On peut faire du shopping.**
One can go shopping.

Town and Country

En ville, il y a…	In town, there is / are…
• **des distractions**	entertainment
• **des magasins**	shops
A la campagne, il y a…	In the country, there is / are…
• **des fermes**	farms
• **des animaux**	animals
La ville est…	The town is…
• **animée**	lively
• **bruyante**	noisy
La campagne est…	The country is…
• **tranquille**	quiet
• **jolie**	pretty
• **trop calme**	too calm

En ville, il y a beaucoup de distractions et il y a toujours quelque chose à faire. Mais, aux heures d'affluence, il y a trop de voitures qui polluent l'air.
In town, there's a lot of entertainment and there's always something to do. But, at rush hour, there are too many cars, which pollute the air.

A la campagne, il n'y a pas de transports en commun et c'est difficile de faire du shopping. Mais, l'air est pur et les paysages sont beaux.
In the country, there's no public transport and it's hard to go shopping. But, the air's pure and the scenery's beautiful.

The Imperfect Tense

The imperfect tense is used to talk about what 'used to' happen in the past. Firstly, you need to know the **nous** form of the present tense, for example:

* **Nous avons**   We have
* **Nous travaillons**   We work
* **Nous prenons**   We take

Take off the **-ons** ending and add the following endings:

Je travaillais	I used to work
Tu travaillais	You used to work
Il / Elle travaillait	He / She used to work
Nous travaillions	We used to work
Vous travailliez	You used to work
Ils / Elles travaillaient	They used to work

The only exception is **être**, which takes the same endings but uses **ét-** as the stem:

J'étais	I was
Tu étais	You were
Il / Elle était	He / She was
Nous étions	We were
Vous étiez	You were
Ils / Elles étaient	They were

Il y a cent ans, ma ville était industrielle, et il y avait beaucoup d'usines.

One hundred years ago, my town used to be industrial and there used to be a lot of factories.

Les hommes travaillaient dans les usines ou dans les mines.

The men used to work in the factories or in the mines.

Les femmes restaient à la maison et elles faisaient le ménage.

The women used to stay at home and (used to) do the housework.

The imperfect is also often used for descriptions in the past tense. For example:

* **L'homme avait une longue barbe et il portait un costume noir.**
  The man had a long beard and he was wearing a black suit.
* **Il faisait très beau et le soleil brillait.**
  The weather was very nice and the sun was shining.

It's also used to say what you 'were' doing. For example:
* **Qu'est-ce que tu faisais?**
  What were you doing?
* **Je faisais de la natation à la piscine.**
  I was swimming at the pool.

Useful Verbs

acheter	to buy
faire du shopping	to do some shopping
visiter	to visit
voyager	to travel
conduire	to drive
marcher	to walk
sortir	to go out
travailler	to work
chercher	to look for
trouver	to find
se trouver	to be situated

Quick Test

1 Say / write it in English:
   a) **Ma ville se trouve dans le nord-ouest de la France.**
   b) **C'est une grande ville industrielle.**
   c) **Il y a beaucoup de magasins et un vieux château.**
   d) **Il travaillait dans une usine.**
2 Say / write it in French:
   a) My town is situated in the south of England.
   b) You can visit the shopping centre and the market.
   c) The town is very noisy and polluted.
   d) They used to finish work at 6 o'clock.

Being Environmentally Friendly

My Local Environment

l'environnement	environment	un quartier	area (of a town)
un arbre	tree	une rivière	river
bruyant	noisy	le trottoir	pavement
calme	calm	une usine	factory
un champ	field	la circulation	traffic
la colline	hill	les déchets	waste
un espace vert	green belt	la paix	peace
une ferme	farm	les papiers	litter
une fleur	flower	pollué	polluted
la fumée	smoke	propre	clean
un incendie	fire	une poubelle	bin
la lumière	light	sale	dirty

Ma ville est calme et tranquille. Il y a beaucoup de jardins publics avec des fleurs et des arbres. L'air est propre.
My town is calm and quiet. There are lots of parks with flowers and trees. The air is clean.

Ma ville est sale et industrielle. Il y a beaucoup d'usines et de circulation. L'air est pollué.
My town is dirty and industrial. There are a lot of factories and traffic. The air is polluted.

Mon village est joli. Mais le week-end des touristes laissent tomber des papiers par terre et la rivière devient polluée.
My village is pretty. But at the weekend tourists drop litter and the river's becoming polluted.

Useful Verbs

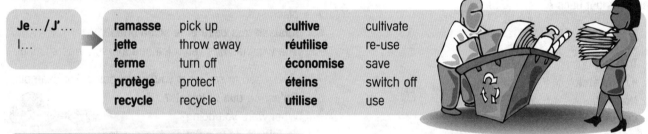

Je… / J'… I…	ramasse	pick up	cultive	cultivate
	jette	throw away	réutilise	re-use
	ferme	turn off	économise	save
	protège	protect	éteins	switch off
	recycle	recycle	utilise	use

Looking After the Environment

Je ramasse des papiers sur le trottoir.
I pick up litter from the pavement.

Je ferme le robinet pour économiser de l'eau quand je me brosse les dents.
I turn off the tap to save water when brushing my teeth.

Je recycle le verre, le carton, le plastique et les boites.
I recycle glass, cardboard, plastic and tins.

Au supermarché, il y a trop d'emballages. Je n'utilise plus de sacs en plastique.
At the supermarket there's too much packaging. I don't use plastic bags anymore.

Dans ma ville, il y a un centre de recyclage. Nous avons des poubelles spéciales pour recycler les journaux et les bouteilles.
In my town, there's a recycling centre. We have special bins for recycling newspapers and bottles.

Je cultive des fruits et des légumes dans le jardin et je ne jette pas de déchets que je peux utiliser pour faire du compost.
I cultivate fruit and vegetables in the garden and I don't throw away waste that I can use to make compost.

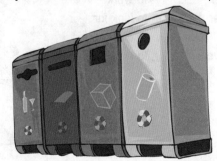

Being Environmentally Friendly

Environmental Problems and Solutions

Il y a trop de voitures. Les gaz d'échappement polluent l'air.
There are too many cars. Exhaust fumes pollute the air.

Aux heures d'affluence, il y a beaucoup d'embouteillages.
At rush hour there are a lot of traffic jams.

Les transports en commun ne sont pas très utilisés.
Public transport is not well used.

Il faut encourager les gens à abandonner leurs voitures. On peut aller au travail à pied.
We must encourage people to stop using their cars. You can walk to work.

Il faut développer les transports en commun.
We must develop public transport.

Il faut créer des zones piétonnes et des pistes cyclables.
We must create pedestrian zones and cycle lanes.

Dans certaines villes, les voitures sont interdites au centre-ville. La pollution est donc diminuée.
In some towns, cars are not allowed in the centre. Pollution is therefore reduced.

The Passive

Verbs usually have an active subject. For example, in the sentence, 'The dog bit the man', the dog is the subject of the verb because the dog is the one that's doing something (the biting).

The sentence can be re-arranged to, 'The man was bitten (by the dog)', and it then becomes a passive sentence (the subject is passive, and can be taken out). Here's another example:
- I wrote the poem. (*active*)
- The poem was written (by me). (*passive*)

As in English, you form the passive in French by using the verb **être** (to be) in the correct tense, followed by the past participle. For example:
- **La pollution est diminuée.**
  Pollution is reduced.
- **Les sacs seront réutilisés.**
  Bags will be re-used.
- **La pollution est causée par les gaz d'échappement.**
  Pollution is caused by exhaust fumes.

Note that the past participle is treated as an adjective and has to agree with the first noun. For example, **la pollution** is feminine so you need **-e** on the past participle **causé**. **Les sacs** are masculine plural and so you add **-s** to the past participle **réutilisé**.

Quick Test

1 Say / write it in English:
  a) Ma ville est bruyante.
  b) Il y a des fleurs dans le parc.
  c) J'éteins la lumière.

2 Say / write it in French:
  a) I recycle glass and paper.
  b) We must use the bus.
  c) The air is polluted by smoke.

Current Problems Facing the Planet

Global Issues

Here are some useful words for talking about issues affecting the world:

la consommation	consumption	le pétrole	crude oil
le charbon	coal	la pluie acide	acid rain
la couche d'ozone	ozone layer	sans plomb	unleaded
le déboisement	deforestation	le réchauffement de la terre	global warming
les détritus	waste		
l'effet de serre	the greenhouse effect	renouvelable	renewable
l'électricité	electricity	les ressources	resources
l'essence	petrol	surpeuplé	overpopulated
le gaz carbonique	carbon gas	un tremblement de terre	earthquake
la guerre	war	le trou	hole
le monde	the world	la vague	wave
mondial	worldwide	l'énergie nucléaire	nuclear energy
la Terre	Earth	l'énergie solaire	solar power
les ordures	rubbish	l'énergie éolienne	wind power

Useful Forms of the Conditional Tense

You already know how useful the conditional tense of the verb **vouloir** is (**je voudrais**), but the verbs **pouvoir**, **devoir**, **falloir** and **valoir** are also very useful in the conditional tense. For example:

- **On pourrait** One / We could, might
- **On devrait** One / We should, ought
- **Il faudrait** One / We should, really must
- **Il vaudrait** It would be worth

On devrait utiliser les transports en commun.
We ought to use public transport.

On pourrait développer des énergies renouvelables.
We could develop renewable energy.

Il faudrait protéger la planète.
We really must protect the planet.

Il vaudrait mieux interdire les voitures au centre-ville.
It would be worthwhile banning cars from the town centre.

Useful Verbs

sauver	to save	réduire / diminuer	to reduce
disparaitre	to disappear	gaspiller	to waste
protéger	to protect	supprimer	to abolish
construire	to build	améliorer	to improve
détruire	to destroy	augmenter	to increase
endommager	to damage	conserver	to conserve, save
produire	to produce		
nettoyer	to clean	fournir	to provide
créer	to create	menacer	to threaten

On pourrait supprimer les sacs en plastique.
We could abolish plastic bags.

On ne devrait pas construire de nouvelles routes.
We shouldn't build new roads.

Current Problems Facing the Planet

Endangered Species

les espèces menacées	endangered species
la baleine	whale
le blaireau	badger
la chauve-souris	bat
le dauphin	dolphin
l'éléphant	elephant
le guépard	cheetah
les oiseaux	birds
l'ours	bear
le panda	panda
le phoque	seal
les poissons	fish
le renard	fox
le rhinocéros	rhino
le tigre	tiger
le singe	monkey

Le tigre est en danger de disparaître.
The tiger is in danger of disappearing.

La pollution de l'eau tue les poissons.
Water pollution kills fish.

Le réchauffement de la terre menace les ours polaires.
Global warming threatens polar bears.

On ne devrait pas chasser les baleines.
We shouldn't hunt whales.

Il faut protéger les espèces menacées.
We should protect threatened species.

Sharing Your Concerns

Je me sens concerné(e) par...		
I feel concerned about...	la guerre	war
	le terrorisme	terrorism
	la pauvreté	poverty
	la famine	famine
	l'insécurité	crime

En Afrique les gens meurent de faim.
In Africa people are dying of hunger.

Des personnes innocentes sont tués.
Innocent people are being killed.

On pourrait supprimer les dettes du Tiers Monde pour combattre la pauvreté.
We could cancel the debts of the Third World to fight poverty.

Using 'En train de...' and 'Sur le point de...'

En train de means 'in the process of (doing something)'.
For example:

* **Certaines espèces sont en train de disparaître.**
  Certain species are in the process of disappearing.
* **Le gouvernement est en train d'agir.**
  The government is in the process of taking action.

Sur le point de means 'to be about to (do something)'. For example:

* **Nous sommes sur le point de gaspiller les ressources naturelles.**
  We're about to waste natural resources.

Quick Test

1. Say / write it in English:
   a) **L'effet de serre est dangereux.**
   b) **Il faut protéger les animaux.**
   c) **L'énergie solaire n'est pas chère.**

2. Say / write it in French:
   a) I'm concerned about poverty.
   b) We should protect tigers.
   c) We are about to destroy the planet.

Celebrations in the Home

Celebrations

C'est quand?	When is it?	**l'anniversaire**	birthday	**le baptême**	Christening
		une boum	party	**les fiançailles**	engagement
au printemps	in Spring	**un jour férié**	bank holiday	**les noces**	(silver) anniversary
en été	in Summer	**les feux d'artifice**	firework display	**(d'argent)**	
en automne	in Autumn	**un bal**	a dance	**une carte**	card
en hiver	in Winter	**un défilé**	procession	**un cadeau**	present
en mars /	in March /	**le mariage**	wedding	**des bougies**	candles
octobre	October	**la naissance**	the birth	**des lumières**	lights
		la mort	the death	**des chansons**	songs

Special Holidays

le nouvel an	New Year		**la fête nationale**	Bastille Day
la Saint-Sylvestre	New Year's Eve		**le quatorze juillet**	14th July
Noël	Christmas		**Diwali**	Diwali
la veille de Noël	Christmas Eve		**Aid**	Eid
l'arbre de Noël	Christmas tree		**Hannoukah**	Hanukkah
le père Noël	Father Christmas		**le nouvel an chinois**	Chinese New Year
Pâques	Easter			

Useful Verbs

On… You… →		
envoie	send
souhaite	wish
offre	give
donne	give
décore	decorate
chante	sing
danse	dance
attend	wait for
jeûne	fast
mange	eat
boit	drink
met	put on
allume	light
reçoit	receive
fête	celebrate

A Noël, on achète des cadeaux, on envoie des cartes, on décore la maison et on mange trop.
At Christmas, we buy gifts, send cards, decorate the house and eat too much.

Je reçois des cartes et des cadeaux.
I receive cards and presents.

Le quatorze juillet, il y a un défilé et le soir il y a un bal dans la rue avec des feux d'artifice.
On the 14th July, there's a procession and in the evening a street party and firework display.

A Diwali, on offre des cadeaux, on allume la maison et on mange des choses sucrées.
At Diwali, we give presents, light up the house and eat sweet things.

A Hannoukah, on allume une bougie chaque soir et on joue aux jeux. On mange des crêpes et des beignets.
At Hanukkah, we light a candle each evening and play games. We eat pancakes and doughnuts.

Celebrations in the Home

Reflexive Verbs in the Perfect Tense

All reflexive verbs (e.g. **se lever**, **se coucher**) take **être** in the perfect tense. Here's the perfect tense of the reflexive verb **s'amuser** ('to have a good time') in full:

Je me suis amusé(e)	I had a good time
Tu t'es amusé(e)	You had a good time
Il s'est amusé	He had a good time
Elle s'est amusée	She had a good time
Nous nous sommes amusé(e)s	We had a good time
Vous êtes amusé(e)(s)(es)	You had a good time
Ils se sont amusés	They had a good time
Elles se sont amusées	They had a good time

Au nouvel an, on a fait le réveillon et je me suis couchée très tard.
At New Year, we had a party and I went to bed very late.

A la fin du Ramadan, je me suis habillé de mes nouveaux vêtements pour fêter l'Aid.
At the end of Ramadan, I got dressed in my new clothes to celebrate Eid.

Au nouvel an chinois, on a nettoyé la maison et on a mis de nouveaux vêtements. On a mangé un grand repas en famille. Nous nous sommes amusés.
At Chinese New Year, we cleaned the house, and put on new clothes. We ate a large family meal. We had a good time.

Direct Pronouns in the Perfect Tense

Normally, past participles of verbs that take **avoir** in the perfect tense don't change. A very tricky bit of grammar (which even French people often get wrong) is making the past participle agree when there's a direct pronoun in front of **avoir**.

Remember, the direct pronoun **le** means 'him' or 'it'; **la** means 'her' or 'it' and **les** means 'them'. For example:
- **Je la déteste**   I hate her.
- **Je les respecte**   I respect them.

When you put **la** or **les** in front of **avoir**, the past participle agrees with the pronoun. For example:
- **Merci pour la carte. Je l'ai reçue hier.**
  Thanks for the card. I got it yesterday.
- **Il m'a offert des bonbons. Je les ai déjà mangés.**
  He gave me some sweets. I've already eaten them.

Quick Test

1 Say / write it in English:
   a) **On envoie des cartes à Noël.**
   b) **Il a allumé les bougies.**
   c) **Elle a reçu beaucoup de cadeaux.**

2 Say / write it in French:
   a) I like celebrating my birthday.
   b) I ate too many chocolates.
   c) I found them delicious.

Celebrations in the Home

Cooking

l'alimentation	food
la cuisine	cooking
le plat	dish
la spécialité	speciality
des ingrédients	ingredients
Ça se mange avec…	It's eaten with…
C'est fait avec…	It's made with…
épicé / piquant	spicy
doux	mild, sweet

Le couscous est un plat qui est la spécialité de l'Afrique du nord.
Couscous is a dish, which is a speciality of North Africa.

C'est fait avec de la viande (souvent de l'agneau), des légumes, des oignons, des tomates et des épices.
It's made with meat (often lamb), vegetables, onions, tomatoes and spices.

Ça se mange avec du thé à la menthe.
It's eaten with mint tea.

Life and Celebrations in Togo

J'habite au Togo en Afrique.
I live in Togo in Africa.

Aujourd'hui c'est le baptême de ma petite sœur.
Today is my little sister's baptism.

Le baptême est célébré dans une petite salle à l'église.
The baptism is celebrated in a small room at the church.

Tout le monde revient manger chez nous.
Everyone comes back to our house to eat.

On fait la cuisine dehors parce qu'il fait si chaud.
The cooking is done outside because it's so hot.

Dans notre jardin, on garde des animaux comme des moutons.
In our garden, we keep animals like sheep.

Traditional Dress in Martinique

Les filles portent des robes en coton.
The girls wear cotton dresses.

D'habitude, on porte des bijoux comme des boucles d'oreille et un collier.
Usually, they wear jewellery such as earrings and a necklace.

On met généralement un chapeau coloré.
They normally put on a colourful hat.

On porte le costume traditionnel pendant le carnaval.
The traditional costume is worn during the carnival.

The Pluperfect Tense

When you want to say what *had* happened you need to use the pluperfect tense. It's formed by using the imperfect tense of **avoir** or **être** with the past participle. For example:

* **Je suis arrivé à l'aéroport mais j'avais oublié mon passeport.**

  I arrived at the airport (*perfect tense*) but I had forgotten (*pluperfect*) my passport.

Here is the pluperfect form of the verb **manger** in full:

J'avais mangé	I had eaten
Tu avais mangé	You had eaten
Il / Elle avait mangé	He / She had eaten
Nous avions mangé	We had eaten
Vous aviez mangé	You had eaten
Ils / Elles avaient mangé	They had eaten

Quand je suis rentrée, ils avaient déjà mangé les chocolats.

When I got home, they had already eaten the chocolates.

Il avait fait le couscous avant notre arrivée.

He had made the couscous before we arrived.

The verb **partir** takes **être** instead of **avoir**. Here is the pluperfect form of **partir** in full:

J'étais parti(e)	I had left
Tu étais parti(e)	You had left
Il était parti	He had left
Elle était partie	She had left
Nous étions parti(e)s	We had left
Vous étiez parti(e)(s)	You had left
Ils étaient partis	They had left
Elles étaient parties	They had left

Il était parti sans moi.
He had left without me.

Traditions

Dans la Creuse, au centre de la France, je suis resté chez des amis pendant un festival qui s'appelle la Saint-Cochon.
In the Creuse in central France I stayed with some friends during a festival called la Saint-Cochon.

J'ai mangé des saucisses de porc. Mes amis avaient préparé les saucisses la veille.
I ate pork sausages. My friends had made the sausages the day before.

A la fin de la soirée, j'étais fatigué. On avait dansé, on avait chanté, on avait joué aux jeux avec les enfants.
At the end of the evening I was tired. We had danced, sung and played games with the children.

Selon la légende, le festival a commencé pour chasser le diable quand une jeune fille du village avait refusé de l'épouser.
According to legend, the festival began in order to chase away the Devil when a young girl of the village had refused to marry him.

Quick Test

1 Say / write it in English:
   a) **Le costume traditionnel est joli.**
   b) **La spécialité de la région est délicieuse.**
   c) **J'avais oublié son anniversaire.**

2 Say / write it in French:
   a) She had gone without him.
   b) The girls wear traditional jewellery.
   c) It's eaten with red wine.

Practice Questions

Reading

1 Read the sentences below and match them to the statements that follow.

A Quand il fait froid en hiver, je mets un pullover au lieu de mettre le chauffage central.

B J'éteins toujours la lumière quand je quitte une pièce.

C Aujourd'hui, en France, seule une bouteille sur trois est recyclée. C'est une honte.

D Je recycle les journaux. Cela permet de sauver des forêts.

E Je ferme le robinet quand je me brosse les dents et je me douche au lieu de prendre un bain.

F J'achète toujours des biscuits emballés dans du carton, plutôt que dans du plastique.

a) Saving electricity ⬜

b) Saving water ⬜

c) Recycling paper ⬜

d) Too much packaging ⬜

e) Avoiding using the central heating ⬜

f) Recycling glass ⬜

2 In the passage below, Patrick talks about his town. Read the passage and answer the questions that follow in English.

> Caen se trouve dans le nord-ouest de la France près de Rouen. Il y a un centre commercial, une piscine, un stade, un théâtre, un cinéma et un musée. On peut faire du sport, faire des promenades à la campagne, faire du shopping.
>
> En ville on peut faire du shopping, il y a toujours quelque chose à faire. Je n'aime pas la campagne. Je préfère la ville parce que la campagne est trop tranquille, il n'y a rien à faire. Il n'y a pas de transport en commun. A l'avenir je voudrais habiter dans un grand appartement à New York, parce que j'adore faire du shopping.

a) Where exactly is Caen?

_____

b) What can you do there?

_____

c) What does Patrick say about the countryside?

_____

d) Where does he want to live in the future and why?

_____

Speaking

3 Give a full response to each of the questions below in French. Say your answer out loud.

a) Où habites-tu?

b) Fais une description de ta maison.

c) Comment est ta ville ou ta région?

d) Qu'est-ce que tu fais pour protéger l'environnement?

Writing

4 You're writing about your plans to make your town more environmentally friendly. Write about each of the following in French.

a) Say what you think are the main problems with your local environment.

....

....

....

b) Describe what you think should be done to overcome these problems.

....

....

....

c) Describe where you'd like to live in the future.

....

....

....

5 You're writing about your plans for the future, including details about your ideal or dream house. Write about each of the following in French.

a) Say what your plans are for the future and why.

....

....

....

b) Say where you would like to live in the future and why.

....

....

....

c) Describe your ideal house.

....

....

....

What School is Like

School Subjects

l'allemand	German	**le français**	French	**la religion**	RE
l'anglais	English	**la géographie**	geography	**la technologie**	technology
l'art dramatique	drama	**l'histoire**	history	**les sciences**	science
la biologie	biology	**l'informatique**	IT	**les travaux manuels**	craft subjects
la chimie	chemistry	**l'instruction civique**	citizenship	**l'EPS (l'éducation**	PE
le dessin	art	**les maths**	maths	**physique et**	
l'éducation physique	PE	**la musique**	music	**sportive)**	
l'espagnol	Spanish	**la physique**	physics		

Pronouns

When you're asked your opinion of your subjects, you can make your answer sound more interesting and natural by using pronouns:

- **Le** – as well as meaning 'the' (masculine) – is a pronoun meaning 'him' or 'it'.
- **La** – as well as meaning 'the' (feminine) – is a pronoun meaning 'her' or 'it'.
- **Les** – as well as meaning 'the' (plural) – is a pronoun meaning 'them'.

Que penses-tu du français?
What do you think of French?

J'aime le français. Je le trouve intéressant.
I like French. I find it interesting.

J'adore la musique. Je la trouve amusante.
I love music. I find it enjoyable.

Je n'aime pas les sciences. Je les trouve difficiles.
I don't like science subjects. I find them difficult.

Giving Opinions

Use these adjectives to give positive opinions:

super / génial	great
intéressant	interesting
facile	easy
amusant	funny, enjoyable
utile	useful
le prof est sympa	the teacher's nice
je suis fort(e) en…	I'm good at…

Use these adjectives to give negative opinions:

nul	rubbish
ennuyeux / barbant	boring
difficile	hard, difficult
affreux	awful, dreadful
inutile	useless
le prof est sévère	the teacher's strict
je suis faible en…	I'm not very good at…

Useful Verbs

apprendre	to learn	**épeler**	to spell	**passer**	to sit (an exam)
commencer	to start	**étudier**	to study	**perdre**	to lose
décrire	to describe	**faire attention**	to pay attention	**porter**	to wear
dessiner	to draw	**faire les devoirs**	to do homework	**poser une question**	to ask a question
dire	to say	**finir**	to finish, to end	**punir**	to punish
échouer	to fail	**gagner**	to win	**quitter**	to leave
écouter	to listen	**lire**	to read	**répondre**	to answer
écrire	to write	**obéir**	to obey	**réussir**	to succeed, pass
enseigner	to teach	**parler**	to speak		

In School

une école	school	un examen	exam	le papier	paper
un collège	11–15 school	la pause-déjeuner	lunch break	une règle	ruler
un lycée	15–18 school	la récréation	break	un règlement	rule
une école primaire	primary school	le trimestre	term	un stylo	pen
une école maternelle	a nursery	les grandes vacances	the long / summer holidays	un tableau noir	a blackboard
un bulletin	school report	l'appel	register	un tableau blanc	a whiteboard
un échange	an exchange	le stylo / le bic	ball-point pen	un atelier	workshop
un / une élève	pupil	un cahier	exercise book	un centre sportif	sports centre
un emploi du temps	timetable	un crayon	pencil	une cantine	canteen
une épreuve	test	une gomme	rubber	un laboratoire	lab
les notes	marks, results	un livre	book	une salle de classe	classroom
les études	studies	un manuel	textbook	une cour	playground

Describing Your School

Mon collège s'appelle le Collège Renoir. Il y a environ huit cent élèves.

My school is called Collège Renoir. There are about 800 pupils.

Les bâtiments sont assez modernes. Il y a un gymnase et une bibliothèque, mais il n'y a pas de piscine.

The buildings are quite modern. There's a gym and a library, but there's no swimming pool.

Les cours commencent à huit heures et demie et ils finissent à quatre heures et demie.

Lessons start at 8.30 and finish at 4.30.

Je préfère l'histoire parce que je la trouve très intéressante. Et le prof est sympa.

I prefer history because I find it very interesting. And the teacher's nice.

Je déteste le dessin parce que le prof est barbant et je le trouve trop difficile. Je ne suis pas très fort en dessin.

I hate art because the teacher's boring and I find it hard. I'm not very good at art.

Which Class Are You In?

Je suis en…	**sixième**	year 7	**troisième**	year 10	**première**	year 12
I am in…	**cinquième**	year 8	**seconde**	year 11	**terminale**	year 13
	quatrième	year 9				

Quick Test

1 Say / write it in English:
   a) J'adore le dessin mais je n'aime pas l'histoire.
   b) Je suis forte en biologie. Je la trouve facile.
   c) Les cours commencent à neuf heures moins vingt.

2 Say / write it in French:
   a) I don't like English because it's boring.
   b) I love physics, I find it interesting.
   c) I'm in year 11 and my sister is in year 8.

What School is Like

Talking About School Uniform

l'uniforme scolaire	school uniform	**le collant**	tights	**le chemisier**	blouse
les chaussettes	socks	**le pantalon**	trousers	**le pullover**	jumper
les chaussures	shoes	**la jupe**	skirt	**le blazer**	blazer
les baskets	trainers	**la chemise**	shirt	**la cravate**	tie

Comment est ton uniforme?
What's your uniform like?

Que penses-tu de l'uniforme?
What do you think of the uniform?

Je porte un pantalon gris, des chaussures noires, une chemise blanche et une cravate rouge. Le blazer est bleu marine.
I wear grey trousers, black shoes, a white shirt and a red tie. The blazer is navy blue.

C'est pratique et confortable. Tout le monde est égal. C'est bon pour la discipline.
It's practical and comfortable. Everyone is equal. It's good for discipline.

Je porte une jupe noire, des chaussettes blanches, un chemisier blanc, un pull vert et un blazer vert. Je ne porte pas de cravate.
I wear a black skirt, white socks, a white blouse, a green jumper and a green blazer. I don't wear a tie.

C'est moche et cher. Tout le monde se ressemble. Je n'aime pas la couleur, c'est trop sombre.
It's ugly and expensive. Everyone looks the same. I don't like the colour, it's too dark.

Je suis française. Je ne porte pas d'uniforme. Pour aller au collège je porte un jean, un sweat-shirt bleu et des baskets blancs.
I'm French. I don't wear a uniform. To go to school, I wear jeans, a blue sweatshirt and white trainers.

Connectives

Here are some useful connectives for linking sentences together:

parce que	because
car	since, because
tandis que	whereas, while
mais	but
cependant	however
donc	so
d'une part	on the one hand
d'autre part	on the other hand
d'ailleurs	moreover

J'aime l'espagnol parce que j'adore passer mes vacances en Espagne.
I like Spanish because I love spending my holidays in Spain.

J'aime la chimie tandis que mon ami préfère la physique.
I like chemistry, whereas my friend prefers physics.

D'une part, l'uniforme est pratique; d'autre part la couleur est moche.
On the one hand, the uniform is practical; on the other hand the colour is awful.

Using 'Depuis'

If you want to say how long you've been doing something for in French, you use the word **depuis** (which also means 'since').

It's used to say that you've been doing something for a period of time and are still doing it. You must use the present tense of the verb. For example:

- **Je joue au tennis depuis cinq ans.**
  I've been playing tennis for five years.
- **J'étudie le français depuis la sixième.**
  I've been studying French since year 7.
- **J'apprends l'informatique depuis deux ans.**
  I've been learning IT for two years.

What School is Like

School Rules

Il faut… You must…	travailler dur	(to) work hard
	faire attention en classe	(to) pay attention in class
Il est permis de… You're allowed…	écouter les autres	(to) listen to others
	respecter les autres	(to) respect others
	faire les devoirs	(to) do homework
	porter l'uniforme	(to) wear uniform
	être poli	(to) be polite

Il ne faut pas… You must not…	parler en classe	(to) talk in class
	porter de bijoux	(to) wear jewellery
	mettre du maquillage	(to) wear make-up
Il est interdit de… It's forbidden…	se battre	(to) fight
	fumer	(to) smoke
	laisser tomber des papiers	(to) drop litter
	être insolent	(to) be insolent / rude

Il ne faut pas manger de chewing-gum en classe.
You mustn't eat chewing gum in class.

Il est strictement interdit de fumer dans les toilettes.
It's strictly forbidden to smoke in the toilets.

Il n'est pas permis de sortir de l'école sans permission.
It's not allowed to leave school without permission.

On ne doit pas sécher les cours.
One mustn't miss lessons.

On ne supporte pas la violence.
Violence isn't tolerated.

Il est interdit d'écrire des graffitis sur les murs de la cantine.
It's forbidden to write graffiti on the canteen walls.

Il ne faut pas être en retard.
You mustn't be late.

The Verb 'Prendre'

The verb **prendre** (to take) is an irregular verb. It isn't an **-re** verb, like **rendre**, **vendre** and **descendre**, so take care when you use it. Here it is in full:

Je prends	I take
Tu prends	You take
Il / Elle prend	He / She takes
Nous prenons	We take
Vous prenez	You take
Ils / Elles prennent	They take

The verbs **comprendre** (to understand) and **apprendre** (to learn) are formed in the same way as **prendre**. For example:

- **Je ne comprends pas la question.**
  I don't understand the question.
- **Elles apprennent l'allemand depuis trois ans.**
  They've been learning German for three years.
- **Nous prenons le déjeuner à la cantine.**
  We have our lunch in the canteen.

Quick Test

1. Say / write it in English:
   a) Je porte une chemise bleue et un pantalon gris.
   b) Mon amie porte des chaussettes tandis que moi je porte un collant.
   c) Il ne faut pas porter des bijoux.

2. Say / write it in French:
   a) I like wearing uniform because it's comfortable.
   b) I don't like the colour, but the blazer is practical.
   c) You mustn't wear make-up.

Pressures and Problems at School

Pressures at School

un / une apprenti(e)	an apprentice
un apprentissage	an apprenticeship
le brevet	exam taken at the end of college
le baccalauréat (le bac)	exam taken at the end of lycée (equivalent of A-levels)
le redoublement	repeating a year
le conseil de classe	meeting of class teachers
le stress	stress
stressant / stressé(e)	stressful / stressed
la formation (professionnelle)	(vocational) training
le bulletin	(school) report
les notes	marks
la moyenne	average mark
extra-scolaire	extra-curricular

Les bonnes notes sont essentielles pour passer dans la prochaine classe.
Good marks are essential to move into the next class.

Les profs ne nous écoutent pas et ils nous donnent trop de devoirs. C'est stressant.
The teachers don't listen to us and they give us too much homework. It's stressful.

Au lycée, je me sens enfermé toute la journée. La vie scolaire est très stressante.
At school, I feel closed in all day. School life is very stressful.

Ma moyenne en maths n'est pas très bonne – seulement 9 sur 20.
My average mark in maths is not very good – only 9 out of 20.

Je vais passer le bac l'année prochaine.
I'm going to sit A-levels next year.

Direct and Indirect Pronouns

Here are the direct pronouns:

me (m')	me
te (t')	you
le (l')	him / it
la (l')	her / it
nous	us
vous	you
les	them

Direct pronouns go in front of the verb. For example:

- **Les profs ne nous écoutent pas.**
  The teachers don't listen to us.
- **Le dessin? Je le déteste.**
  Art? I hate it.
- **Mon amie m'aide beaucoup.**
  My friend helps me a lot.

Here are the indirect pronouns:

me (m')	to me, for me
te (t')	to you, for you
lui	to him / her, for him / her
nous	to us, for us
vous	to you, for you
leur	to them, for them

Indirect pronouns also go in front of the verb, but they're used with verbs that need an indirect object, like **donner** (to give) **offrir** (to offer), **dire** (to say, tell) and **parler** (to talk to). They're used to say something is done 'to' or 'for' someone. For example:

- **Le professeur leur donne trop de devoirs.**
  The teacher gives them too much homework. (The teacher gives too much homework *to* them.)
- **Il lui dit son secret.**
  He's telling him / her his secret. (He's telling his secret *to* him / her.)
- **Il ne lui parle jamais.**
  He never speaks *to* him / her.

Pressures and Problems at School

More Connectives

Here are some more useful connectives:

à cause de	because of	où	where
malgré	in spite of	puisque	since
grâce à	thanks to	dès que	as soon as
quand	when		

Je dois obtenir de bonnes notes puisque je veux devenir vétérinaire.
I must get good marks, since I want to become a vet.

Malgré ses mauvaises notes, elle espère aller à l'université où elle veut étudier la physique.
Despite her bad marks, she hopes to go to university where she wants to study physics.

Grâce à sa formation, on lui a offert un poste.
Thanks to his training, they offered him a job.

Il est difficile de me concentrer en classe à cause du bruit.
It's hard for me to concentrate in class because of the noise.

Stress

Je n'ai pas le temps de faire des activités extra-scolaires.
I don't have time to do extra-curricular activities.

Mes parents me mettent sous trop de pression.
My parents put too much pressure on me.

On travaille tout le temps et on n'a pas de temps pour les loisirs.
We work all the time and we don't have time for leisure activities.

Certains profs ne s'intéressent pas aux élèves.
Some teachers aren't interested in the pupils.

Je veux obtenir un bon emploi donc je dois travailler tout le temps et je vois rarement mes amis.
I want to get a good job so I must work all the time and I rarely see my friends.

Je ne comprends rien en maths. Les explications du prof ne me disent rien.
I understand nothing about maths. The teacher's explanations mean nothing to me.

Dans ma classe, certains élèves parlent trop et ne font pas attention au prof.
In my class, certain pupils talk too much and don't pay attention to the teacher.

Using 'Pour'

As an alternative to **parce que**, you can use **pour** (for) followed by the infinitive, to give a reason for doing something. For example:

- **Je veux aller à l'université pour étudier le français.**
  I want to go to university (in order) to study French.
- **Elle veut faire un stage pour devenir mécanicienne.**
  She wants to do a course (in order) to become a mechanic.

- **Pour obtenir de bonnes notes, il faut travailler très dur.**
  (In order) To get good marks, you have to work very hard.

Quick Test

1. Say / write it in English:
   a) **Mon prof me donne trop de devoirs.**
   b) **Mes parents ne m'écoutent pas.**
   c) **Les activités extra-scolaires sont excellentes.**
2. Say / write it in French:
   a) My friend talks too much in class.
   b) We work all the time.
   c) I'm not interested in vocational training.

Current and Future Jobs

Plans After Finishing School

L'école est une bonne préparation pour la vie active.
School is good preparation for working life.

J'ai l'intention de devenir docteur.
I intend to become a doctor.

Je vais aller au lycée technique parce que je veux travailler comme mécanicien.
I'm going to go to technical college because I want to work as a mechanic.

J'ai envie de travailler à l'étranger plus tard dans la vie.
I want to work abroad later in life.

Jobs

un agent de police	police officer	**un(e) employé(e)**	employee	**un(e) informaticien(ne)**	IT worker
un boucher	butcher	**un épicier**	grocer	**un ingénieur**	engineer
un boulanger	baker	**une mère au foyer**	housewife	**un(e) mécanicien(ne)**	mechanic
un caissier /	cashier	**un homme au foyer**	house husband	**un médecin**	doctor
une caissière		**un facteur**	postman	**un professeur**	teacher
un chauffeur	driver	**un fermier**	farmer	**une secrétaire**	secretary
un coiffeur /	hairdresser	**un garçon**	waiter	**un vendeur /**	shop
une coiffeuse		**une serveuse**	waitress	**une vendeuse**	assistant
un dentiste	dentist	**une hôtesse de l'air**	air hostess	**un vétérinaire**	vet
un directeur /	headteacher,	**un infirmier /**	nurse		
une directrice	manager	**une infirmière**			

When talking about jobs in French, don't use **un** or **une** before the name of the job. For example:

- **Il est infirmier.** — He's a nurse.
- **Elle va devenir médecin.** — She's going to become a doctor.

Why do You Want to do that Job?

Je veux devenir mécanicien parce que j'adore les voitures.
I want to be a mechanic because I love cars.

Je rêve de devenir vétérinaire car les droits des animaux me sont importants.
I dream of becoming a vet because animal rights are important to me.

Je veux devenir médecin pour aider les autres.
I want to become a doctor to help other people.

Je veux travailler dans une ferme parce que j'aime être en plein air et je ne veux pas être enfermé dans un bureau.
I want to work on a farm because I like being in the open air and I don't want to be shut in an office.

Useful Expressions

L'année prochaine	Next year	**Au bout de l'année**	At the end of the year
La semaine prochaine	Next week	**Après deux semaines**	After two weeks
A l'avenir	In the future	**Bientôt**	Soon
Dans deux mois	In two months		

The Conditional Tense

You use the conditional tense when you want to say what *would* happen. You've already used the conditional tense of **vouloir** in the form **je voudrais** (I would like).

To form the conditional tense, you use the same form of the verb as the future tense (usually the infinitive) and then add exactly the same endings as the imperfect tense.

Here's a regular verb in the conditional tense: the verb **jouer** in the infinitive form with the imperfect endings:

Je jouerais	I would play
Tu jouerais	You would play
Il / Elle jouerait	He / She would play
Nous jouerions	We would play
Vous joueriez	You would play
Ils / Elles joueraient	They would play

Now, let's take an irregular verb. The verb **faire** uses the form **fer-** in the future tense, so the conditional form of the verb is as follows:

Je ferais	I would do
Tu ferais	You would do
Il / Elle ferait	He / She would do
Nous ferions	We would do
Vous feriez	You would do
Ils / Elles feraient	They would do

You're quite likely to come across the conditional tense when you meet the word **si** (if). **Si** changes to **s'** before **il**.

Immediately after **si**, you use the imperfect tense, then use the conditional tense in the main clause:

S'il faisait beau, je jouerais au tennis.
If it was fine (imperfect), I would play tennis (conditional).

Si j'étais riche, j'irais en Australie.
If I was rich, I would go to Australia.

Si c'était possible, je deviendrais docteur.
If it was possible, I'd become a doctor.

Saying What You Would Do

S'il travaillait dur, je serais content.
If he worked hard, I'd be pleased.

Si elle portait des bijoux, les profs la puniraient.
If she wore jewellery, the teachers would punish her.

S'il le savait, il serait furieux.
If he knew, he'd be furious.

Si j'avais beaucoup d'argent, je ferais le tour du monde.
If I had lots of money, I'd travel around the world.

Si mes parents gagnaient à la loterie, ils achèteraient une nouvelle maison au bord de la mer.
If my parents won the lottery, they would buy a new house at the seaside.

Quick Test

1. Say / write it in English:
   a) **Je veux devenir ingénieur plus tard dans la vie.**
   b) **Mon ami espère travailler comme vétérinaire.**
   c) **Il irait à l'université, si c'était possible.**
2. Say / write it in French:
   a) I dream of becoming a doctor.
   b) He will soon finish his apprenticeship.
   c) If I had enough money, I'd go to Spain.

Current and Future Jobs

Part-time Work

travailler	to work	**aider**	to help	**commencer**	to begin	
gagner	to earn	**servir**	to serve	**finir**	to finish	
recevoir	to receive	**faire du**	to babysit	**préparer**	to prepare	
obtenir	to obtain	**babysitting**		**répondre**	to answer	
livrer	to deliver	**garder**	to look after			

J'ai un petit job.
I have a part-time job.

Le samedi, je travaille dans un café. Je gagne cinq livres par heure.
On Saturdays, I work in a café. I earn £5 an hour.

Je commence à dix heures et demie et je finis vers quatre heures.
I start at 10.30 and finish about 4.

Je sers les clients et j'aide dans la cuisine.
I serve the customers and I help in the kitchen.

Je fais de temps en temps du babysitting pour mes voisins. Je reçois dix livres.
I sometimes do babysitting for my neighbours. I receive £10.

Je livre des journaux. C'est assez bien payé mais c'est fatigant.
I deliver newspapers. It's quite well paid, but it's tiring.

Using Two Verbs Together

When you want to use two verbs together in the same phrase, there are three possibilities:

1 Some verbs are followed by the infinitive of the second verb, for example:
- **Je veux trouver un petit job.**
  I want to find a part-time job.

Other verbs that are followed by an infinitive include **aimer** (to like), **devoir** (to become) and **pouvoir** (to be able to). For example:
- **Je n'aime pas servir les clients.**
  I don't like serving customers.

2 Some verbs are followed by **à** and then the infinitive, for example:
- **Je commence à travailler à huit heures.**
  I start working at 8 o'clock.

Other verbs that are followed by **à** and then the infinitive include **encourager** (to encourage), **continuer** (to continue) and **aider** (to help). For example:
- **J'aide le patron à préparer les sandwichs.**
  I help the boss to prepare sandwiches.

3 Some verbs are followed by **de** and then the infinitive, for example:
- **J'essaie de gagner de l'argent pour acheter une voiture.**
  I'm trying to earn some money to buy a car.

Other verbs that are followed by **de** and then the infinitive include **décider** (to decide), **finir** (to finish) and **arrêter** (to stop). For example:
- **Je vais arrêter de livrer des journaux.**
  I'm going to stop delivering newspapers.

Current and Future Jobs

Pocket Money

Avec mon argent de poche, j'achète… With my pocket money, I buy…	de quoi manger	things to eat	des bijoux	jewellery
	des vêtements	clothes	des jeux-vidéo	computer games
	des CD	CDs	des affaires scolaires	things for school
	des magazines	magazines	des cadeaux	presents
	du maquillage	make-up	des cartes	cards

Je veux économiser de l'argent pour… I want to save money to…	partir en vacances	go on holiday
	m'offrir un vélo	treat myself to a bike
	acheter un ordinateur	buy a computer

Mes parents me donnent de l'argent. Je reçois dix livres par semaine.
My parents give me money. I receive £10 a week.

Je dois aider à la maison pour avoir de l'argent.
I have to help in the house to get money.

Saying You Need Something

The French don't have a verb meaning 'to need'. They use the expression **avoir besoin de**, meaning 'to have need of'. For example:

- **J'ai besoin d'un emploi.**   I need a job.
- **Elle a besoin d'un vélo.**   She needs a bike.

More Irregular Verbs

The verbs **recevoir** (to receive) and **servir** (to serve) are irregular. Here's the verb **recevoir** in full:

Je reçois	I receive
Tu reçois	You receive
Il / Elle reçoit	He / She receives
Nous recevons	We receive
Vous recevez	You receive
Ils / Elles reçoivent	They receive

Other irregular verbs in this group include **dormir** (to sleep), **sortir** (to go out), **partir** (to set off), **sentir** (to smell, feel) and **mentir** (to tell lies).

The verb **servir** belongs to a small group of common irregular verbs, which are all formed in the same way:

Je sers	I serve
Tu sers	You serve
Il / Elle sert	He / She serves
Nous servons	We serve
Vous servez	You serve
Ils / Elles servent	They serve

Quick Test

1. Say / write it in English:
   a) Je travaille dix heures par semaine.
   b) Il n'aime pas garder son petit frère.
   c) Ma sœur m'encourage à trouver du travail.
2. Say / write it in French:
   a) I earn five pounds an hour.
   b) She wants to find a job.
   c) I want to save money and buy some computer games.

Current and Future Jobs

Work Experience

Here are some verbs that you'll probably want to use in the perfect tense to talk about what you did during work experience:

J'ai travaillé	I worked	**J'ai téléphoné**	I phoned	**J'ai réparé**	I repaired
J'ai commencé	I started	**J'ai préparé**	I prepared, made	**J'ai servi**	I served
J'ai fini	I finished	**J'ai tapé**	I typed	**J'ai écrit**	I wrote
J'ai voyagé	I travelled	**J'ai fait**	I did, made	**J'ai lu**	I read
J'ai aidé	I helped	**J'ai photocopié**	I photocopied		

L'année dernière, j'ai fait un stage pratique.
Last year, I did some work experience.

J'ai travaillé dans une école / une banque / un magasin / un bureau.
I worked in a school / bank / shop / office.

Pendant mon stage, j'ai travaillé sur ordinateur, j'ai répondu au téléphone et j'ai photocopié des documents.
During my work experience, I worked on computer, answered the phone and photocopied documents.

Giving Your Opinion

To give your opinion of your work experience, the imperfect tense would be most appropriate:

Dans l'ensemble, le stage était…
Overall, my work experience was…

intéressant	interesting	**ennuyeux**	boring
amusant	enjoyable, funny	**une perte de temps**	a waste of time
utile	useful	**inutile**	useless
fatigant	tiring		

Mes collègues étaient…
My colleagues were…

sympa	nice	**gentils**	kind
agréables	pleasant	**antipathiques**	unfriendly
travailleurs	hard-working	**impolis**	impolite, rude

Le patron était…
The boss was…

compréhensif	understanding	**paresseux**	lazy
aimable	helpful	**sévère**	strict
efficace	efficient	**désagréable**	unpleasant

You might have made decisions about your future as a result of your work experience.

A cause de mon stage, j'ai décidé que je ne veux pas travailler dans une banque plus tard dans la vie.
Because of my experience, I've decided I don't want to work in a bank later in life.

Grâce à mon stage, je suis certain(e) que je voudrais devenir professeur.
Thanks to my experience, I'm sure that I'd like to become a teacher.

Current and Future Jobs

Advantages and Disadvantages of Different Jobs

Les Avantages	Advantages
C'est bien payé.	It's well paid.
Mes collègues sont sympa.	My colleagues are pleasant.
Je m'entends bien avec le patron.	I get on well with the boss.
J'ai beaucoup de responsabilités.	I have a lot of responsibilities.
J'aime le contact avec le public.	I like meeting the public.
C'est un travail important.	It's an important job.
Les Inconvénients	**Disadvantages**
Le salaire n'est pas bon.	It's not well paid.
Les heures de travail sont longues.	The hours are long.
C'est fatigant et monotone.	It's tiring and monotonous.
Le trajet est trop long.	The journey is too long.
Le patron est trop sévère.	The boss is too strict.

Using the Correct Tense

Here's a brief reminder of when to use the different tenses in French.

The imperfect tense is often used to set the scene before an event happened (the event itself is expressed using the perfect tense). For example:

- **J'allais au travail quand j'ai vu l'accident dans la rue.**
  I was going to work (*imperfect*) when I saw the accident (*perfect*) in the street.

When using the conditional tense, don't forget that **si** is followed by the imperfect tense.

- **Si elle travaillait plus dur, elle gagnerait plus d'argent.**
  If she worked (*imperfect*) harder, she would earn (*conditional*) more money.

When using the future tense, watch out for **quand**. For example:

- **Quand je serai plus âgé, je deviendrai conducteur de train.**
  When I'm older, I'll become a train driver.

Remember that **depuis** is often used with the present tense in French. For example:

- **Je travaille dans la banque depuis deux ans.**
  I've been working in the bank for two years.

Quick Test

1. Say / write it in English:
   a) **J'ai gagné vingt livres.**
   b) **Le stage était utile et intéressant.**
2. Say / write it in French:
   a) She found a job in a shop.
   b) I helped the children a lot.

Practice Questions

Reading

1 Read the passages by Christian, Frédéric, Salma and Abdul below and answer the questions that follow.

Je déteste l'ambiance dans mon collège. C'est très stressant. Pour les profs, seulement les bonnes notes et les devoirs sont importants. On travaille trop tout le temps et on n'a pas assez de temps pour faire des loisirs. Je ne peux pas sortir le week-end parce qu'on a trop à faire.

Frédéric

J'aime bien mon école. J'ai beaucoup d'amis et on s'amuse bien. Mais la bibliothèque est trop petite et on n'a pas assez d'équipements sportifs.

Christian

L'école est très importante parce qu'il faut réussir à ses examens pour avoir un bon emploi. Mais il est souvent très difficile de bien travailler en classe parce que beaucoup d'élèves ne s'intéressent pas aux cours et ils n'écoutent pas le prof. Ils passent tout le temps à parler et c'est très énervant pour moi.

Salma

A mon école, les professeurs ne sont pas très gentils. Ils ne s'intéressent pas aux élèves et ils ne nous écoutent pas. Je ne m'entends pas très bien avec eux. C'est triste.

Abdul

a) Who doesn't think the teachers are very nice? ....

b) Who would like better facilities at school? ....

c) Who complains about other pupils' bad behaviour? ....

d) Who wants to do well in exams? ....

e) Who doesn't like the atmosphere in the school? ....

f) Who finds school stressful? ....

g) Who has a good time with friends at school? ....

h) Who doesn't have enough time to do leisure activities? ....

Speaking

2 Give a full response to each of the questions below in French. Say your answer out loud.

a) Comment est ton école?

b) Décris une journée typique.

c) Comment est ton uniforme?

d) Quelle est ta matière préférée? Pourquoi?

e) Que veux-tu faire après l'école? Pourquoi?

f) Quel travail est-ce que tu feras à l'avenir?

Writing

3 Imagine you're at a new school. Write about each of the following in French.

a) Describe the school as it is now.

....

....

....

b) Say what subjects you like and dislike, and explain why.

....

....

....

c) Write about your attitude to school rules and uniform and say what new buildings you'd like.

....

....

....

4 You're writing about your ideal job. Write about each of the following in French.

a) Say what job you'd like to do in the future and why.

....

....

....

b) Say what you need to do in order to get your ideal job.

....

....

....

c) Say where you'd like to work and why.

....

....

....

Word Bank

un / une ado	teenager	une dégustation	food tasting
les affaires	business	la demi-pension	half board
de l'ail	garlic	démodé	old-fashioned
aller bien / mieux	to be fine / better	dépenser	to spend (money)
amer / amère	bitter	déprimé	depressed
une annonce	small advert	dérouler en bas / en haut	to scroll up / down
annuler	to cancel	la déviation	diversion
l'antenne	aerial	deviner	to guess
atterrir	to land	un diplôme	qualification
un auteur	author / writer	discuter	to discuss
avertir	to warn	un distributeur automatique	cash dispenser
se baigner	to swim	doué	talented
un baiser	a kiss	la douleur	pain
bête	stupid	un drapeau	flag
bien cuit	well done (steak)	un droit	a right
bien équipé	well equipped	les droits de l'homme	human rights
la bijouterie	jewellery shop	effacer	to erase
une boîte aux lettres électronique	electronic mail box	emballer	to wrap
un boulot	work / job (slang)	empêcher	to prevent / stop
le bureau des renseignements	information office	un enlèvement	kidnapping
un cadre	manager	l'ennui (m)	trouble
un caméscope	camcorder	s'ennuyer	to get bored
le canard	duck	une enquête	enquiry
un car de ramassage scolaire	school bus	s'entrainer	to train
une carafe	jug	envahir	to invade
un carnet	notebook	épais(se)	thick
une carrière	career	épuiser	to exhaust
la carte d'identité	identity card	un escalier roulant	escalator
un casque	helmet	un espoir	a hope
un casse-croûte	snack	l'esprit	wit, mind
une casserole	saucepan	exclus	excluded
une ceinture	belt	la faculté	faculty / university
un champignon	mushroom	fana de	fan of
le chemin de fer	railway	la farine	flour
la climatisation	air conditioning	une femme de ménage	cleaner
un comptable	accountant	feuilleter	to leaf through
compter sur	to rely on	les fléchettes	darts
le comptoir	counter	un fleuriste	florist
un concours	competition	le foie	liver
la connaissance	knowledge	une foire d'exposition	trade fair
un conseil	advice	gâcher	to spoil
la console de jeu	games console	un genre	a type / kind
une côtelette	a chop	un gigot d'agneau	leg of lamb
un couloir	corridor	hors d'haleine	out of breath
coupable	guilty	une huître	oyster
couramment	fluently	une ile	island
le courrier électronique	email	un immeuble	multi-storey building
une crevette	a prawn	imprimer	to print
cru	raw	les incivilités	anti-social behaviour
déchirer	to tear	inconnu	unknown
décoller	to take off	inquiet	worried
déçu	disappointed	un / une instituteur / institutrice	primary school teacher
défense de	no… / not allowed	l'instruction religieuse	RE
faire défiler	to scroll	ivre	drunk

un jardinier	gardener	la racaille	scum
un jeu (de société)	(board)game	ralentir	to slow down
un jouet	toy	la réclame	advertisement, offer
juif	Jewish	reconnaissant	grateful
lancer	to throw	redoubler	to repeat a school year
les langues vivantes	modern foreign languages	réduit	reduced
faire du lèche-vitrine	to window shop (display)	réfléchir	to reflect, think
les libertés civiques	civil liberties	remarquer	to notice
une licence	a degree	être remboursé	to get money back
licencier	to sack	renoncer	to give up
un lieu	a place	la rentrée	start of school year
la location de voitures	car hire	reprendre connaissance	to regain consciousness
la loi	the law	un réseau	a network
lourd	heavy	respirer	to breathe
un magnétoscope	a video recorder	la retenue	detention
la maison de la presse	newsagents	la retraite	retirement
mal équipé	badly equipped	le rouge à lèvres	lipstick
la marée	tide	un routier	truck driver
marquer (un but)	to score (a goal)	le sable	sand
en avoir marre	to be fed up	saignant	rare (steak)
la maternelle	nursery	salé	salty
les matières grasses	fat	sans ressources	poor
de mauvaise humeur	in a bad mood	sauvegarder	to safeguard
mener	to lead	savoureux	tasty
mentir	to lie	sens interdit	no entry
mettre de l'argent à côté	to put money aside	sens unique	one-way street
se mettre en route	to set off	un souci	a concern
la mi-temps	half-time	une station balnéaire	seaside resort
monoparental	single parent	une station de ski	ski resort
une mosquée	mosque	surchargé	overcrowded
les mots croisés	crossword	un tableau (blanc interactif)	(interactive white) board
un niveau	a level	une tâche	a task
une noix	nut	se taire	to be quiet
une odeur	smell	taper	to type
une offre d'emploi	job offer	un tatouage	tattoo
l'orchestre	stalls	un témoin	witness
un ouvre-boîte	tin-opener	un tire-bouchon	corkscrew
la page d'accueil	homepage	un tiroir	drawer
un panneau	a sign	un toit	roof
un passage à niveau	level crossing	une tournée	a tour
à peine	scarcely	la Toussaint	All Saints' Day (1 November)
pénible	painful		
la pension complète	full board	tousser	to cough
une piqûre	injection / sting	traduire	to translate
plein	full	le traitement de texte	word processing
la plongée sous-marine	underwater diving	une truite	trout
à point	medium (steak)	tuer	to kill
un poumon	lung	vide	empty
le pourboire	tip	du vinaigre	vinegar
la prise	plug / socket	vivre	to live
la promotion	special offer	le voisin	neighbour
le / la propriétaire	the owner	un volet	a shutter
en provenance de	from (train's starting point)		
le pull à capuche	a 'hoody'		

Answers

Quick Test
Page 9
1. **a)** It's Wednesday 6th July 2008. **b)** The time is quarter past ten in the morning.

Lifestyle 1

Quick Test
Page 11
1. **a)** My father's 39 years old. **b)** My sister has a rabbit. **c)** I have 2 sisters but I don't have any brothers.
2. **a)** Mon père a 45 ans. **b)** Ma mère a un frère. **c)** Je suis fils / fille unique.
Page 13
1. **a)** My father has short hair. **b)** My mother wears glasses. **c)** I am of medium height.
2. **a)** Mon père a les cheveux longs. **b)** J'ai les cheveux bruns et les yeux bleus. **c)** Comment s'appelle ton frère?
Page 15
1. **a)** I am nice and funny. **b)** My sister is clever and shy. **c)** My parents are serious and impatient.
2. **a)** Mon père est intelligent mais un peu sérieux. **b)** Mon frère est plus paresseux que moi. **c)** Ma sœur est moins égoïste que mon frère.
Page 17
1. **a)** I get on well with her. **b)** They often argue with me. **c)** She is in love but unhappy.
2. **a)** Mon meilleur ami est animé mais un peu fou. **b)** Je rêve de me marier avec ma petite amie. **c)** Ma sœur est plus polie que mon frère.
Page 19
1. **a)** I'm going to marry my ideal partner. **b)** I'm going to have 3 children. **c)** She intends to work in the USA.
2. **a)** Mon amie rêve d'épouser Johnny Depp. **b)** Mon partenaire idéal est plus riche que moi. **c)** L'amour est plus important qu'un mariage.
Page 21
1. **a)** I want to protest against crime. **b)** You should join in the demonstration against war. **c)** She intends to do voluntary work for a charity.
2. **a)** Il veut protester contre le chômage. **b)** J'ai l'intention de réaliser mes ambitions. **c)** On devrait respecter les droits de l'homme.

Practice Questions Pages 22–23
1. **a)** intelligente **b)** paresseux **c)** généreuse **d)** sévère
2. **a)** i)–iii) **Any three from:** Long hair; Blue eyes; Medium height; Taller than Laura. **b)** i)–ii) **In any order:** They like the same music; They like shopping. **c)** 2 months **d)** He won't go out. / He wants to stay in all the time.
3. **Example answers: a)** Je m'appelle…, mais mes amis

2. **a)** Je m'appelle Pierre. Ça s'écrit P-i-e-r-r-e. **b)** Pardon, où est le CDI?

m'appellent… . C'est mon surnom. **b)** J'ai quinze ans, mais je vais avoir bientôt seize ans. **c)** Je suis assez petit, j'ai les cheveux bruns et les yeux verts. **d)** On dit que je suis intelligent, amusant et sportif, mais je suis paresseux de temps en temps. **e) i)** J'ai un petit frère qui a neuf ans. **ii)** Je ne m'entends pas bien avec lui parce qu'il est casse-pieds.

4. **Example answers: a)** Il s'appelle Jacques Dubonnet. Il a 25 ans. Il est assez grand. Il a les cheveux longs et raides et les yeux noisette. Il aime le sport mais il n'aime pas la musique. Il est intelligent, mais un peu égoïste. *His name is Jacques Dubonnet. He's 25. He's quite tall. He has long, straight hair and hazel eyes. He likes sport but he doesn't like music. He is clever but a bit selfish.*

b) Il est fils unique. Il est divorcé. Il a une petite amie qui s'appelle Tania et qui a 21 ans. Il s'entend bien avec la mère de Tania mais le père de Tania déteste Jacques. Il pense qu'il est paresseux, impoli et méchant. *He's an only child. He's divorced. He has a girlfriend called Tania who's 21. He gets on well with Tania's mother but her father hates Jacques. He thinks he's lazy, rude and nasty.*

c) Il se dispute avec le père de Tania et il se bat avec lui dans le café. Il finit à l'hôpital avec un bras cassé. Le père de Tania refuse de lui permettre de sortir avec Jacques. Que faire? *He argues with Tania's father and fights with him in the café. He ends up in hospital with a broken arm. Tania's father refuses to let her go out with Jacques. What is to be done?*

5. **Example answers: a)** Après l'école, je veux voyager et voir le monde. J'ai l'intention de visiter l'Australie parce que les gens sont sympa et je voudrais voir des kangourous. Je vais aller à l'université parce que je veux devenir docteur. *After school, I want to travel and see the world. I intend to visit Australia because the people are friendly and I would like to see kangaroos. I'm going to go to university because I want to become a doctor.*

b) Mon partenaire idéal est beau et grand. Il a les cheveux bruns et les yeux verts. Il est honnête et généreux / Ma partenaire idéale est belle et grande. Elle a les cheveux bruns et les yeux verts. Elle est honnête et généreuse. *My ideal partner is good-looking and tall. He / She has brown hair and green eyes. He / she is honest and generous.*

c) A l'avenir, je rêve de me marier à l'âge de 25 ans. Je veux avoir des enfants parce que j'adore les bébés. Je veux avoir une fille et un garçon. *In the future, I dream of getting married at the age of 25. I want to have children because I love babies. I want to have a girl and a boy.*

Lifestyle 2

Quick Test
Page 25
1. **a)** I'm very hot. **b)** I played football. **c)** They went shopping.
2. **a)** Elle a vu le match. **b)** Il promène le chien tous les jours.

c) Il va au travail en bus.
Page 27
1. **a)** He no longer takes drugs. **b)** She only has 2 euros. **c)** My father didn't understand anything.

2. **a)** Elle ne fume plus. **b)** La drogue mène à la violence. **c)** Je ne vais jamais nulle part.

Page 29
1. **a)** I'd like some potatoes. **b)** She buys / is buying a kilo of pears. **c)** He chose a strawberry ice cream.
2. **a)** Je voudrais des framboises. **b)** Elle veut le poulet-frites. **c)** Il voudrait un kilo de tomates.

Page 31
1. **a)** I'd like to taste / try seafood. **b)** He eats fruit every day. **c)** My sister never has vegetables.
2. **a)** Elle mange très lentement. **b)** Avez-vous des bananes? **c)** J'en voudrais deux.

Page 33
1. **a)** I play football once a week. **b)** I've just played squash. **c)** I'm about to go to the sports centre.
2. **a)** Je joue au hockey depuis 3 ans. **b)** Il va à Paris pour 3 jours. **c)** En jouant au foot, il a marqué un but.

Practice Questions Pages 34–35
1. **Pour:** A, F, G; **Contre:** B, C, D, E.
2. **a)** Annie **b)** Philippe **c)** Morgane **d)** Annie **e)** Morgane **f)** Philippe
3. **Example answers: a)** Je mange des fruits et des légumes parce que c'est bon pour la santé. **b)** J'ai horreur de ça – c'est dangereux pour les poumons. **c)** Je bois de la bière de temps en temps, mais pas trop souvent. **d)** Je fais du vélo et je fais du jogging. **e)** J'aime faire du sport. Je joue au tennis chaque semaine et j'adore le foot.
4. **Example answers: a)** Je suis en assez bonne forme parce que je fais du sport régulièrement. Le mardi, je vais à la piscine où je fais de la natation. Samedi dernier, je suis allé au gymnase pour faire de la musculation. C'était amusant mais fatigant. *I'm in quite good shape because I do sport regularly. On Tuesdays I go to the pool where I swim. Last Saturday I went to the gym to do some bodybuilding. It was fun but tiring.*
   b) J'essaie de manger équilibré. J'aime les fruits et les légumes parce qu'il faut en manger cinq portions par jour. J'évite le chocolat et les bonbons parce qu'il y a trop de sucre dedans. *I try to eat a balanced diet. I like fruit and vegetables because you should eat 5 portions a day. I avoid chocolate and sweets because there is too much sugar in them.*
   c) A l'avenir, je ne vais jamais fumer parce que c'est trop dangereux et je vais boire de l'alcool avec modération. *In the future, I'm never going to smoke because it is dangerous and I'm going to drink alcohol in moderation.*
5. **Example answers: a)** Le week-end dernier j'ai fait mes devoirs. Pour me relaxer j'ai regardé la télé et j'ai lu un bon livre. *Last weekend I did my homework. To relax, I watched TV and I read a good book.*
   b) J'ai mangé des fruits et des légumes parce que j'aime garder la forme. Pour le dîner samedi soir, j'ai mangé du poulet avec des pommes de terre et j'ai bu de l'eau minérale. Mais j'ai pris un dessert – un gros gâteau au chocolat! *I ate fruit and vegetables because I like to keep healthy. For my evening meal on Saturday evening, I ate chicken and potatoes and I drank mineral water. But I had a dessert – a big chocolate cake!*
   c) J'ai fait de la natation à la piscine. Puis j'ai joué au badminton avec mes amis. Après, j'ai fait du shopping et j'ai acheté une nouvelle jupe. *I went swimming at the swimming pool. Then I played badminton with my friends. Afterwards, I went shopping and I bought a new skirt.*

Leisure

Quick Test
Page 37
1. **a)** I went out with my friends. **b)** She doesn't like scary films at all. **c)** They sang in a choir.
2. **a)** Je voudrais voir un film d'amour. **b)** Il est rentré tard. **c)** Ils ont vu le film puis ils sont allés au café.

Page 39
1. **a)** Do you want to eat at the restaurant? **b)** He's just learnt to play the piano. **c)** Whose coat is this?
2. **a)** Tu veux jouer au foot? **b)** C'est à qui, cette maison? **c)** C'est à eux mais je n'aime pas le jardin.

Page 41
1. **a)** I'd like to pay with this credit card. **b)** She's looking for a T-shirt at the market. **c)** This shop is too big.
2. **a)** Cet ascenseur ne marche pas. **b)** Elle préfère ces fraises-ci. **c)** Le vin est très cher.

Page 43
1. **a)** I put on a white shirt. **b)** She doesn't like the denim jacket. **c)** She prefers this wool one.
2. **a)** Cette jupe est trop étroite. **b)** Elle préfère ceux-ci en blanc. **c)** Ce pull est trop cher.

Page 45
1. **a)** I appreciate soaps. **b)** She bought a new mobile phone. **c)** They often send texts.
2. **a)** Je voudrais un lecteur MP3. **b)** Je télécharge de la musique ce qui est facile. **c)** Sa sonnerie est énervante.

Page 47
1. **a)** I often surf the Internet. **b)** He buys books on French websites. **c)** He downloads music, even though it's illegal.
2. **a)** Je déteste les publicités pour les voitures. **b)** Ma sœur a le meilleur ordinateur. **c)** Bien qu'il soit nouveau, l'ordinateur est lent.

Page 49
1. **a)** I'm going to the seaside. **b)** He always goes to India. **c)** She likes Spanish food.
2. **a)** Je veux faire de la voile. **b)** Elle n'aime pas aller au Pays de Galles. **c)** Les filles sont hollandaises.

Page 51
1. **a)** I'm going to Italy for a week. **b)** Before arriving, I ate a sandwich. **c)** After eating, I drank a coffee.
2. **a)** Je veux rester jusqu'au 9 juillet. **b)** Les garçons sont en retard. **c)** Ils ont l'intention de partir vers 4 heures.

Page 53
1. **a)** A room for one person. **b)** I'd like to stay for 2 nights. **c)** The pedestrian is injured.
2. **a)** Je veux rester pour 4 nuits. **b)** Elle a perdu son porte-monnaie. **c)** La vue est superbe.

Page 55
1. **a)** It's sunny. **b)** It will be hot. **c)** On Monday, it / the weather was bad.
2. **a)** Il fait du vent et il fait froid. **b)** Elle aime le soleil. **c)** Il fera du brouillard.

Page 57
1. **a)** Go straight on and turn left at the lights. **b)** Where is the nearest restaurant?
2. **a)** Pour aller à la plage? **b)** A quelle heure arrive le train?

Answers

Leisure (cont.)

Practice Questions Pages 58–59

1. **a)** La France **b)** l'Italie **c)** les États-Unis **d)** l'Espagne
   e) l'Angleterre **f)** l'Allemagne
2. **a)** The Alps. **b)** To ski. **c)** One week. **d)** By coach. **e)** It was long and tiring. **f)** Small hotel. **g)** Went to the bar and drank (hot) chocolate. **h)** Cold and snowy.
3. **Example answers: a)** J'aime me relaxer. J'adore bronzer et nager mais j'aime aussi faire du shopping pour acheter des souvenirs. **b)** J'ai passé deux semaines en Italie avec mes parents. **c)** J'ai visité des monuments, j'ai passé beaucoup de temps sur la plage et j'ai mangé beaucoup de pizzas. **d)** Il a fait chaud mais un soir il y a eu un orage effrayant.
4. **Example answers: a)** Au mois de juillet, je suis allée à un petit village au bord de la mer en Italie. Il y avait un petit restaurant, une église et un magasin. J'y suis allée en avion et on a loué une voiture pour aller à l'hôtel. *In July, I went to a little village by the sea in Italy. There was a small restaurant, a church and a shop. I went there by plane and we hired a car to get to the hotel.*
   b) On est resté dans un hôtel confortable et propre au centre du village. On a bronzé à la plage et on a fait des excursions dans la campagne. Les vacances étaient très relaxantes. *We stayed in a clean comfortable hotel in the centre of the village. We sunbathed on the beach and went on excursions in the country. The holiday was very relaxing.*

   c) L'année prochaine, je voudrais aller aux Etats-Unis pour visiter la Floride. Je veux visiter les parcs d'attractions et loger dans une villa avec une piscine. *Next year, I would like to go to America to visit Florida. I want to visit the theme parks and stay in a villa with a swimming pool.*
5. **Example answers: a)** Le mois prochain, j'ai l'intention de visiter le bord de la mer avec un groupe d'amis. On va prendre le train parce que c'est assez rapide et pas trop cher. *Next month, I intend to visit the seaside with a group of friends. We're going to go by train because it's quite quick and not too expensive.*
   b) D'abord, on va aller à la plage pour jouer au foot. Après, on va visiter le parc d'attractions parce que j'aime les montagnes russes. On va manger des hamburgers avec des frites parce que c'est rapide et pratique. *First of all, we'll go on the beach to play football. Afterwards, we'll visit the theme park because I like roller coasters. We'll eat hamburgers and chips because it's quick and practical.*
   c) La dernière fois que je suis allé au bord de la mer, j'ai passé une journée catastrophique. Je suis tombé dans la mer et j'ai perdu tout mon argent. Je ne me suis pas amusé du tout. *The last time I went to the seaside I had a disastrous day. I fell in the sea and I lost all my money. I did not have a good time at all.*

Home and Environment

Quick Test
Page 61
1. **a)** I like the kitchen, which is modern. **b)** My brother must clean his room. **c)** My parents often do the gardening. The garden is very attractive.
2. **a)** Ma sœur déteste faire le ménage. **b)** Au rez-de-chaussée, il y a un grand salon et une cuisine. **c)** J'aime passer l'aspirateur mais je fais rarement le repassage.

Page 63
1. **a)** The lounge is between the kitchen and the study. **b)** The carpet is green and red. **c)** The dog is under the bed.
2. **a)** Ma maison se trouve en banlieue. **b)** Je me lève à 7h30 tous les jours. **c)** Je prends le petit déjeuner dans la cuisine.

Page 65
1. **a)** My town is in the north west of France. **b)** It's a big industrial town. **c)** There are a lot of shops and an old castle. **d)** He used to work in a factory.
2. **a)** Ma ville se trouve dans le sud de l'Angleterre. **b)** On peut visiter le centre commercial et le marché. **c)** La ville est très bruyante et polluée. **d)** Ils finissaient le travail à 6 heures.

Page 67
1. **a)** My town is noisy. **b)** There are flowers in the park. **c)** I switch off the light.
2. **a)** Je recycle le verre et le papier. **b)** Il faut prendre le bus. **c)** L'air est pollué par la fumée.

Page 69
1. **a)** The greenhouse effect is dangerous. **b)** It's necessary to protect animals. **c)** Solar energy isn't expensive.
2. **a)** Je m'inquiète de la pauvreté. **b)** Il faut protéger les tigres. **c)** Nous sommes sur le point de détruire la planète.

Page 71
1. **a)** We send cards at Christmas. **b)** He lit the candles. **c)** She received lots of presents.
2. **a)** J'aime fêter mon anniversaire. **b)** J'ai mangé trop de chocolats. **c)** Je les ai trouvés délicieux.

Page 73
1. **a)** The traditional costume is pretty. **b)** The region's speciality is delicious. **c)** I had forgotten his birthday.
2. **a)** Elle était partie sans lui. **b)** Les filles portent des bijoux traditionnels. **c)** Ça se mange avec du vin rouge.

Practice Questions Pages 74–75
1. **a)** B **b)** E **c)** D **d)** F **e)** A **f)** C
2. **a)** The north-west of France, near Rouen. **b)** Sport, walks in the countryside, shopping. **c)** He doesn't like it because it's too peaceful. **d)** In a big apartment in New York because he loves shopping.
3. **Example answers: a)** J'habite au sud de l'Ecosse dans une petite ville tranquille. **b)** Il y a trois chambres. Devant la maison il y a un petit jardin avec des fleurs. Nous avons un grand salon et une petite cuisine moderne. **c)** Ma ville est calme et il n'y a pas beaucoup à faire pour les jeunes. **d)** Je recycle le papier et le verre et j'utilise les transports en commun le plus souvent possible.
4. **Example answers: a)** Dans ma ville, il y a trop de voitures et donc l'air est très pollué. Les rues sont sales parce qu'il y a beaucoup de papiers. *In my town, there are too many cars and so the air is very polluted. The streets are dirty because there is a lot of litter.*
   b) A l'avenir, on devrait créer une zone piétonne au centre-ville. En même temps, il faut développer les transports en

commun. Je veux encourager les gens à recycler le papier et le verre. *In the future, we should create a pedestrian zone in the town centre. At the same time we must develop public transport. I want to encourage people to recycle paper and glass.*

c) Je rêve d'habiter à la campagne. Il n'y aura pas d'embouteillages ou de bruit et je voudrais habiter une petite ferme avec des animaux. *I dream of living in the country. There won't be any traffic jams or noise and I would like to live on a little farm with animals.*

5. **Example answers: a)** Après l'école, je veux voyager et voir le monde. J'ai l'intention de visiter l'Australie parce que je voudrais voir des kangourous. Je vais aller à l'université parce que je veux devenir docteur. *After school, I want to travel and*

see the world. I intend to visit Australia, because I'd like to see kangaroos. I'm going to go to university because I want to become a doctor.*

b) A l'avenir, je rêve d'habiter au bord de la mer en Espagne parce qu'il fait chaud et j'adore la cuisine espagnole. J'aime aussi bronzer. *In the future, I dream of living by the sea in Spain because it's hot and I love Spanish food. I also like sunbathing.*

c) Ma maison idéale est grande avec quatre chambres, trois salles de bains et un beau jardin avec une piscine. Au rez-de-chaussée il y a un grand salon, une cuisine moderne et une salle à manger qui donne sur le jardin. *My ideal house is big with 4 bedrooms, 3 bathrooms and a lovely garden with a pool. Downstairs, there's a big lounge, a modern kitchen and a dining room overlooking the garden.*

Work and Education

Quick Test
Page 77
1. **a)** I love art but I don't like history. **b)** I am good at biology. I find it easy. **c)** Lessons start at 8.40am.
2. **a)** Je n'aime pas l'anglais parce que c'est ennuyeux. **b)** J'adore la physique, je la trouve intéressante. **c)** Je suis en seconde et ma sœur est en cinquième.

Page 79
1. **a)** I wear a blue shirt and grey trousers. **b)** My friend wears socks whereas I wear tights. **c)** You're not allowed to wear jewellery.
2. **a)** J'aime porter l'uniforme parce que c'est confortable. **b)** Je n'aime pas la couleur mais le blazer est pratique. **c)** Il ne faut pas mettre de maquillage.

Page 81
1. **a)** My teacher gives me too much homework. **b)** My parents don't listen to me. **c)** The extra-curricular activities are excellent.
2. **a)** Mon ami parle trop en classe. **b)** Nous travaillons tout le temps. **c)** Je ne m'intéresse pas à la formation professionnelle.

Page 83
1. **a)** I want to become an engineer later in life. **b)** My friend hopes to work as a vet. **c)** He'd go to university if it was possible.
2. **a)** Je rêve de devenir docteur. **b)** Il finira bientôt son apprentissage. **c)** Si j'avais assez d'argent, j'irais en Espagne.

Page 85
1. **a)** I work 10 hours a week. **b)** He doesn't like looking after his younger brother. **c)** My sister encourages me to find work.
2. **a)** Je gagne 5 livres par heure. **b)** Elle veut trouver un travail. **c)** Je veux économiser de l'argent pour acheter des jeux-vidéo.

Page 87
1. **a)** I earned £20. **b)** Work experience was useful and interesting.
2. **a)** Elle a trouvé un travail dans un magasin. **b)** J'ai beaucoup aidé les enfants.

Practice Questions Pages 88–89
1. **a)** Abdul **b)** Christian **c)** Salma **d)** Salma **e)** Frédéric **f)** Frédéric **g)** Christian **h)** Frédéric
2. **Example answers: a)** C'est une grande école avec 1000 élèves. Il y a une bibliothèque moderne. **b)** Les cours commencent à 9h et il y a cinq cours par jour. **c)** Je porte un pantalon noir et une cravate bleue. **d)** J'aime mieux le dessin. C'est intéressant et utile. **e)** J'espère aller à l'université. Je veux étudier les sciences. **f)** Je travaillerai comme dentiste.
3. **Example answers: a)** L'école est assez moderne. Il y a une nouvelle bibliothèque, un centre sportif et un gymnase. Les cours commencent à neuf heures moins le quart et finissent à

trois heures et demie. L'uniforme scolaire est bleu marine et on porte un blazer. *The school is quite modern. There is a new library, a sports centre and a gym. Lessons start at 8.45 and end at 3.30. The uniform is navy blue and we wear a blazer.*

b) J'aime beaucoup le dessin parce que le prof est sympa et j'aime aussi l'histoire parce que c'est utile. En revanche, je n'aime pas du tout les sciences parce que je les trouve trop difficiles. *I like art a lot because the teacher is nice and I also like history because it's useful. On the other hand, I don't like science at all because I find it difficult.*

c) Il y a trop de règles. Les élèves pourraient porter des jeans. On aurait le droit de porter des bijoux. Je voudrais faire construire une nouvelle piscine. *There are too many rules. Pupils could wear jeans. They would be allowed to wear jewellery. I would like to have a new swimming pool built.*

4. **Example answers: a)** Après l'école, je veux devenir docteur parce que j'ai toujours voulu aider les autres. Le problème, c'est que j'ai peur du sang mais je suis forte en sciences et je rêve de gagner beaucoup d'argent. *After school, I want to become a doctor because I've always wanted to help others. The problem is that I am frightened of blood but I'm good at science and I dream of earning lots of money.*

b) Je sais que je dois aller à l'université et donc j'ai besoin de très bons résultats à mes examens. La formation est longue mais je veux vraiment réussir. *I know that I must go to university and so I need very good results in my exams. The training is long but I really want to succeed.*

c) Je crois que j'irai en Afrique pour soigner des enfants malades. Ensuite, je reviendrai en Grande-Bretagne et je commencerai ma carrière. *I think I'll go to Africa to look after sick children. Afterwards, I will come back to Britain and I will start my career.*

Index

A
Abbreviations 9
Accommodation 52
Active lifestyle 25
Adjectives 14, 19
Adverbs 31
Adverts 47
Alcohol 30
Aller 18
Alphabet 7
Après 50
Avant 50
Avoir 12, 24

B
Buses 57
Buying things 41

C
Camping 53
Cars 56
Ce / cette / ces 41
Celebrations 70
Cinema 37
Classes 77
Clothes 42
Colours 7
Comparing people 15
Computers 46
Conditional tense 68, 83
Connectives 9, 78, 81
Cooking 72
Countries 48, 72
Countryside 64

D
Daily routine 63
Dates 6
Days 6
Depuis 78
Describing people 12
Describing your house 60
Devoir 61
Direct pronouns 71, 80
Directions 56
Dont 61
Drinks 28
Drugs 27

E
En 30
En train de... 69
Endangered species 69
Environment 66–67
-er verbs 13
Être 12

F
Faire 60
Family members 10
Films 37
Food 28
Future plans 18, 19
Future tense 55

G
Gender 10
Getting around 51
Global issues 68
Greetings 8

H
Healthy diets 31
Holidays 50
House 62

I
Il faut 20
Imperfect tense 65
Impersonal verbs 45
Inactive lifestyle 25
Indirect pronouns 80
Instructions 56
Intensifiers 15
Internet 46
Invitations 38
-ir verbs 18
Irregular adjectives 40
Irregular verbs 85

J
Jobs 82, 87

L
Leisure 36
Lengths of time 51
Lequel / lequelle 42
Local area 64

M
Mettre 43
Mobile phones 45
Months 6
MP3 players 45
Music 39
Musical instruments 39

N
Nationalities 48
Negatives 26, 27, 30
Numbers 6

O
On 21
Opinions 76, 86

P
Part-time work 84
Passive 67
Pastimes 36
Perfect tense 24, 36, 71
Personality 14
Pets 10
Plans after finishing school 82
Pluperfect 73
Plural 10
Pocket money 85
Possessive pronouns 38
Pour 81
Pouvoir 64
Prendre 79

Prepositions 50, 62
Present participle 32
Problems 53
Pronouns 17, 76
   direct pronouns 71, 80
   indirect pronouns 80
   possessive pronouns 38
   relative pronouns 44

Q
Quantities 29
Question words 9
Questions 52
Qui / que 44, 61

R
-re verbs 17
Reading 39
Recipes 31
Reflexive verbs 16, 71
Relationships 16
Relative pronouns 44
Restaurant 29

S
School rules 79
School subjects 76
School uniform 78
Shopping 40
Shops 40
Singular 10
Smoking 26
Social issues 20, 21
Special holidays 70
Sports 32
Stress 81
Subjunctive 46
Superlative 47
Sur le point de... 69

T
Television 44
Tickets 57
Time 7
Time expressions 25, 32
Town 64
Traditional dress 72
Traditions 73
Trains 57
Travelling 49
Tu 8

U
Using two verbs together 84

V
Venir 37
Vouloir 20
Vous 8

W
Weather 54
Work experience 86

Y
Y 49